British Battlecruisers of World War 1

Operational Log

July 1914 – June 1915

Hugh Harkins

Copyright © 2013 Hugh Harkins

All rights reserved.

ISBN: 1-903630-24-X
ISBN-13: 978-1-903630-24-2

British Battlecruisers of World War 1

Operational Log

July 1914 – June 1915

A CENTURION BOOK

© Hugh Harkins 2013

ISBN 10: 1-903630-24-X
ISBN 13: 978-1-903630-24-2

First Published in the United Kingdom 2013

The Author is identified as the copyright holder of this work under sections 77 and 78 of the Copyright Designs and Patents Act 1988

Published by Centurion Publishing, Glasgow, United Kingdom, G65 9YE

Cover design © Centurion Publishing & Createspace

Page layout, concept and design © Centurion Publishing

The traditional start of chapter on the recto side only has been intentionally disregarded; chapters starting on either the recto or verso side as required in the interests of the environment

All rights reserved. No part of this publication may be reproduced, stored in a retrieval system, transmitted in any form, or by any means, electronic, mechanical, or photocopied, recorded or otherwise without the written permission of the publishers

Dedicated to the Memory of my Nibbler

British Battlecruisers

CONTENTS

	INTRODUCTION	7
1	THE BATTLE CRUISERS AND THE ROAD TO WAR	8
2	THE *GOEBEN* BREAKTHROUGH – AUGUST 1914	27
3	HMAS *AUSTRALIA* IN THE PACIFIC - AUGUST 1914 to JANUARY 1915	44
4	THE NORTH SEA AND ATLANTIC – AUGUST 1914 to 31 DECEMBER 1914	49
5	THE BATTLE OF THE FALKLAND ISLANDS	98
6	THE NORTH SEA AND ATLANTIC – 1 JANUARY to 30 JUNE 1915	118
7	THE FIRST DARDANELLES BOMBARDMENT – NOVEMBER 1914	134
8	HMS *INFLEXIBLE* AT THE DARDANELLES AND AFTER – FEBRUARY to JUNE 1915	137
9	APPENDICES	147
10	GLOSSARY	152
	BIBLIOGRAPHY	153

INTRODUCTION

The purpose of this volume is to provide a detailed log of the operations of the Royal Navy Battle Cruisers and associated units from July 1914 until the end of June 1915. During this time the Battle Cruisers were engaged with elements of the German Fleet on a number of occasions; most notably in the Battle of the Heligoland Bight in August 1914, The Battle of the Falkland Islands in December 1914 and The Battle of the Dogger Bank in January 1915. Only in the Dogger Bank action did the opposing forces Battle Cruisers engage in battle which resulted in a material and strategic defeat for the German High Seas Fleet, albeit at the cost on one British Battle Cruiser severely damaged.

In the Heligoland Bight action on 28 August 1914, the British Battle Cruisers provided support to light forces engaging German Light forces. The result was a defeat for the German Fleet, which now concentrated on strengthening the defenses of the area.

The Battle of the Falkland Islands in December 1914 was a pivotal moment for the advocates of the Battle Cruiser concept. Battle Cruisers successfully engaged and defeated enemy Armoured Cruisers and Light Cruisers; the very role for which they had been designed.

Intended as an operational history of the employment of the British Battle Cruisers, it is not the intention of this volume to go into the details of the rights or wrongs of the Battle Cruiser concept. It will suffice for the purposes of this volume to state that the designs emerged as an evolution or replacement of the Armoured Cruiser. Not tied to any single role, the new Battle Cruisers were capable of operating as independent units hunting down enemy Cruisers, as in the Falklands battle, or in larger scale operations with the Battle Fleet; scouting ahead with the potential to operate as a fast wing of the Battle Fleet in a fleet action. For this latter role, later in the war, the British Battle Cruisers in particular proved unsound in design, tactics or a combination of both.

During the first year of the War, British Battle Cruisers would be employed in all of the above roles.

1

THE BATTLE CRUISERS AND THE ROAD TO WAR

Towards the end of the 19th Century and into the first few years of the 20th Century, the two power standard that the Royal Navy was being prepared for was in most circles considered to be war with France and Russia in an Alliance. With the Entente this seemed far less likely, but new enemies were emerging with Germany and the United States of America both vying for second place in the naval powers league, a position which France was fast relinquishing. History has shown that Germany took the number two sea power position, with the United States taking third place. For Britain, a real problem would emerge with a German-United States Alliance. It was evident within the British establishment that "evanescent quarrels" with the United States were likely in the future, and that a "parricidal war" with the United States could not be ruled out as that young nation had many territorial ambitions; some of which would inevitably bring her into conflict with the British Empire if she were to act on them, not least her long standing plans to invade and subjugate the self-Governing Dominion of Canada.

Japan was a fast rising naval power in the Far East, but she had an alliance with Great Britain, which would have a constraining effect on any ambitions the United States may have harboured about becoming involved in a confrontation between Britain and any other major power. However, it was Lord Fisher's belief, not without foundation, that of the three largest naval powers following Britain; France, Germany and the United States, that any combination of two of these powers "would hesitate" to attack Britain, such was Britain's naval supremacy in the first years of the new Century. He went on to state that if any combination of two of these powers had attacked Britain, then "they would have been defeated" by British Naval Power without "the assistance of our Japanese allies." That said, while confident in British naval supremacy at that time, Fishers writings make it clear that he was aware that the future of that supremacy would be under threat by the growing naval strength of other naval powers on both sides of the Atlantic.

In the first few years of the 20th Century a revolution was taking place in design of Capital Ships leading to the December 1906 launch of HMS *Dreadnought*, the first of the new "all-big-gun" Capital ships, which would be colloquially known from that time onwards as Dreadnoughts.

A memorandum "Admiralty Work and Progress" issued by the then First Lord, Lord Cawder on 30 November 1905 stated "At the present time strategic requirements necessitate an output of four large armoured ships annually." An announcement in Parliament in July 1906 stated that only three Battleships (Cawders large armoured ships) were to be included in the then current program. Among the reasons cited for withdrawal from the planned four Battleships was that there had been a temporary halt in Battleships construction on the Continent of Europe following the advent of HMS *Dreadnought*, the first all-big-gun Battleship, and the planned *Invincible Class* all-big-gun Armoured Cruisers (these vessels had not yet been designated Battlecruisers). Foreign navies had been forced to reevaluate their construction programs to compete with the revolutionary new type of Battleship, which was not only much heavier armed, but in most areas better armoured and faster than the existing status quo vessels which would soon have the indignation of being labeled 'Pre-Dreadnought' Battleships.

The reduction from four to three Battleships caused much disquiet among certain circles within the establishment, particularly as it came so soon after the ascension to power of the new Liberal government, who were being outright accused of jeopardising the security of the United Kingdom. At the time of this memorandum, the assumption within press circles was that only two of these ships were to be Battleships and two Armoured Cruisers. It has to be remembered though that at this time there was no public conception of what the *Invincible* Class actually was (they would later be termed Battle Cruisers) and the general fallback description within the press was they were modern Armoured Cruisers. Fisher saw these vessels very differently, more of a fast Battleship as borne out by his writings "… with its 6 knots superiority of speed to everything afloat, and the biggest guns alive. The *Invincible's* are as a matter of fact, perfectly fit to be in the line of battle with the battle fleet, and could more correctly be described as battleships, which thanks to their speed, can drive anything afloat off the seas."

"Panic at the present time is stupid. The Board of Admiralty is not to be frightened by paper programs. They will cautiously do all that they judge necessary to secure the existing naval supremacy of this country: the moment that is threatened they will throw caution to the winds and out build our rivals at all costs".

HMS *Invincible* pre-war.

HMS *Invincible*

The name sake of the first of the new class of ship that would eventually become known as the Battle Cruiser or Battlecruiser (Battle Cruiser was the official tern), HMS *Invincible*, was ordered in 1906, laid down at the Armstrong Elswick Works Ltd shipyard in Newcastle-upon-Tyne on 2 April 1906 and launched just over a year later on 13 April 1907. She was built at a cost of £1,765,515.00 and commissioned on 20 March 1909. She was not the first of the new 'Large Armoured Cruisers' to be completed; HMS Inflexible having commissioned in October the previous year.

Prior to her completion Captain Mark E. F. Kerr was appointed to command her on 8 September 1908. *Invincible* left the dock on Tyneside on 26 September and on 21 October, just under a month later, she departed Tyneside bound for Spithead and arrived at the naval base at Portsmouth on 23 October to prepare for a program of sea trials, which were conducted in the English Channel from 4 to 11 November that year.

On 28 December 1908, *Invincible* was struck by the Collier *ODEN*. She suffered extensive damage, which included buckling of a number of beams and hull frames and some (5) bottom ship plates were damaged. As a result of this collision and repairs, ultimately she was delayed in her completion of her fitting out at Heburn-on-Tyne, where she arrived on 23 January. She was declared complete on 16 March 1909 (also reported as 6 March). Two days later she sailed from the Tyne for Portsmouth but suffered another mishap during the voyage when she was in a collision with the Brigantine *MARY ANN*, resulting in severe damage to the *MARY ANN*. *Invincible*, therefore, remained on station until a Lifeboat from Yarmouth reached the scene to tow the *MARY ANN* into port. *Invincible* then continued to Portsmouth and was officially commissioned into the Royal Navy on 20 March 1909, being allocated to the 1st CS (Cruiser Squadron), 1 Division of the Home Fleet. The following month *Invincible* participated in fleet exercises, and again in June 1909. June 1909 also saw *Invincible* take part in the Spithead Review on the 12th of the month and a review of the fleet at Spithead on 2 July that year.

On 17 August 1909, *Invincible* entered into refit at Portsmouth until 17 January 1910. She again entered refit at Portsmouth on 3 August 1910 until October that year, with a further period in refit between 13 March and 2 June 1911. During this period she received a change of command, with Captain R. P. F. Purefoy taking over on 28 March 1911. Although some records state that this refit lasted until 2 June 1911, other records show that she re-commissioned at Portsmouth on 16 May 1911. Over the course of the next year and a half she underwent three further spells in refit. The first of these lasted from 15 December 1911 to 11 January 1912, the second from 16 April 1912 until 4 May 1912 and the third from 1 November 1912 until 28 November that year. During this time, she underwent another change of command when Captain M. Culme-Seymour took over on 1 May 1912.

When the 1st Cruiser Squadron became the 1st BCS (Battle Cruiser Squadron) *Invincible* remained with the Squadron under its new designation. While in Stokes Bay on 17 March 1913, *Invincible* was involved in a collision with the Royal Navy Submarine *C.34*, but sustained no serious damage. She remained with the 1st Battle Cruiser Squadron until August 1913 when she was transferred to the 2nd Battle Cruiser Squadron in the Mediterranean Sea under the command of Captain H. B. Pelly. After a few months with the 2nd Battle Cruiser Squadron she entered refit at Malta on 30 October 1913, completing on 5 November that year. However, she returned to Home Waters in December 1913 and entered into an extensive refit in March 1914, with this being completed in July that year. This major refit saw her electric power mountings being converted to hydraulic. Another change of command occurred when Captain C. M. de Bartolme was appointed to take command on 1 August 1914 as the Royal Navy was about to take up its war positions. *Invincible* was re-commissioned into the 2nd Battle Cruiser Squadron literally on the eve of war, on 3 August 1914, and the following day Great Britain declared war on Germany.

Top: HMS *Indomitable* was the first of the Class of warship to enter service when she was commissioned into fleet service on 1 June 1908. Above: HMS *Inflexible*, the last of the 3 *Invincible* Class.

HMS *Indomitable*

HMS *Invincible's* sister ship, HMS *Indomitable*, was ordered in 1906 as the second of the three *Invincible* Class, although she would have the distinction of becoming the first to enter service. She was laid down at Fairfield Shipbuilding and Engineering Company at Govan Shipyard on the River Clyde on 1 March 1906; launched on 16 March 1907 and commissioned on 1 June 1908 (some sources claim she was commissioned on 20 June 1908) with her first Captain, Captain H. G. King Hall. Built at a cost of £1,752,339.00, Indomitable had the same power plant and armament as *Invincible*. Her high speed, graceful lines, size and position as a symbol of British naval might ensured that she was inevitably selected to sail H.R.H. Prince George V on a visit Canada for the Quebec Tercentenary celebrations, which was effectively her first official task, departing the United Kingdom in company with the Armoured Cruiser HMS *Minotaur* on 15 July 1908, and returning on 2 August that year. The desire to showcase the new warship to the world resulted in delays to her completion. She returned to Chatham on 8 August and entered dockyard hands to be completed, which was effected by 28 October 1908 when she was transferred to the Nore Division of the Home Fleet. Here she remained until transferring to the 1st Cruiser Squadron on its formation in March 1909. She was allocated as Flagship of the 1st Cruiser Squadron on 26 July 1909, flying the Flag of Rear Admiral S. Colville, with the Flag of Captain C. M. de Bartolome as Captain.

Indomitable underwent a refit at Chatham between July and August 1910. On 3 January 1911, Captain A. A. M. Duff took command and she again entered refit from 13 February until 1 April 1911. On 24 February 1911, while still undergoing refit, she was allocated as Flagship of Rear Admiral Lewis Bayly. She entered into another refit from 20 November 1911 until 14 February 1912, following which she re-commissioned on 21 February as Flagship of the 2nd Cruiser Squadron, flying the flag of Rear Admiral Sir George Warrender, with new Captain, Captain G. H. Baird. She was allocated to the 1st Cruiser Squadron with Captain F. W. Kennedy commanding in December 1912, and was still with this formation when it changed to the 1st BCS (Battle Cruiser Squadron) in early 1913. On 27 August 1913, she was allocated to join the 2nd Battle Cruiser Squadron and moved to the Mediterranean to serve with the Mediterranean Fleet.

In late July 1914, she entered into refit at Malta and on the outbreak of war, less than a week later, was readied for participation in the search for the German Battlecruiser SMS *Goeben* and the Light Cruiser SMS *Breslau*.

The powerful 12 inch guns from *Indomitable's* 'P' and 'Q' turrets are positioned across the decks. LOC

HMS *Inflexible*

The third and last of the three *Invincible* Class, HMS *Inflexible*, was ordered from John Brown shipyard on the Clyde. She was laid down on 5 February 1906, launched on 26 June 1907 and Commissioned at Chatham on 20 October 1908, with Captain Henry H. Torlesse, who had been appointed as her Captain in June 1908. Following commissioning she was allocated to the Nore Division of the Home Fleet. In the days following commissioning she was damaged during gunnery trials resulting in her being docked at Chatham for refit and repairs between late October 1908 and January 1909. *Inflexible* was transferred to the 1st Cruiser Squadron of the Home Fleet when this unit formed in March 1909.

As the new Invincible Class of warships were considered the show-pieces of the Fleet, *Inflexible* was allocated as Admiral of the Fleet Sir E. H. Seymour's Flagship for a visit to New York, USA to mark the Hudson-Fulton Celebrations, returning to Home Waters in October 1909; entering into refit on the 11th of that month, with the refit being completed in December that year. Captain C. L. Napier took command of her on 14 December 1909. She underwent another refit at Chatham between 23 August and 12 October 1910.

Inflexible was involved in a collision with the *Bellerophon Class* Battleship HMS *Bellerophon* off Portland on 26 May 1911, resulting in some damage to *Inflexible*, requiring repairs in dockyard hands. She again entered refit at Chatham from 9 October to 25 November 1911, during which she received some modifications, including raising her forward funnel by some six feet. On 21 November, while still under refit, Captain R. F. Phillimore took command of her. From November 1911, she was allocated as the temporary Flagship of the 1st Cruiser Squadron while HMS *Indomitable* was undergoing refit. One date of 18 November 1911 has been put forward as the date she was allocated as Flagship, although she would not have took up full Flag duties until she left refit one week later. She remained Flagship of 1st Cruiser Squadron until 8 May 1912 when the new *Lion* Class Battle Cruiser HMS *Lion* took over the role. On this date Captain R. S. Phipps-Hornby took command. In October 1912 she entered refit at Chatham and re-commissioned under the Command of Captain A. N. Loxley at Chatham on 5 November, being allocated as Flagship fort Admiral Sir A. Berkeley-Milne, Commander in Chief of the Mediterranean Fleet, taking *Inflexible* to the warmer climes of the Mediterranean Sea where she remained at the outbreak of war in August 1914.

HMS *Indefatigable*

Following on from the 3 Invincible *Class*, three *Indefatigable Class* Battle Cruisers were ordered, one of which would enter service with the fledgling Royal Australian Navy, while the remaining two would be commissioned into the Royal Navy, although one of these, HMS *New Zealand* was paid for by this country after which the ship was named. The *Indefatigable Class* were larger and heavier than the proceeding *Invincible Class*, but retained the 8 x 12-in gun main armament, although the arrangement was altered from that of the *Invincible* Class.

The first of the 3 *Indefatigable Class*, HMS *Indefatigable*, was laid down on 23 February 1909, launched on 28 October that year and commissioned at Devonport on 24 February 1911, commanded by Captain A.C. Leveson who had been appointed to command her on 17 January. She was allocated to the 1st Cruiser Squadron, serving with this formation until it was renamed the 1st Battle Cruiser Squadron in January 1913. On 24 February she received a change of command when Captain C. F. Sowerby was appointed to take command of her. She moved to the Mediterranean to join the Mediterranean Fleet in December 1913, serving with the 2nd Battle Cruiser Squadron. In the hours before the outbreak of war between Great Britain and Germany on 4 August 1914, she joined the search For the German Battlecruiser *Goeben* and the Light Cruiser *Breslau*.

Top: HMS Indefatigable. Above: The forward 12 inch gun turret on the Indefatigable Class Battlecruiser HMS New Zealand. The Indefatigable Class had the same main armament as the Invincible Class, although the arrangement was altered to allow all eight guns to be fired on a broadside.

HMS *New Zealand* during her launch at the Fairfield Shipbuilding yards in Govan, Glasgow, on 1 July 1911.

HMS *New Zealand*

In 1909, the then New Zealand Prime Minister announced that his nation would fund construction of a single Battle Cruiser of the *Indefatigable* Class for service with the Royal Navy. This ship, HMS *New Zealand*, was ordered in 1909, laid down at Fairfield Shipbuilding Company on the River Clyde on 20 June 1910, launched on 1 July 1911 and commissioned in 1912. Her build cost was £1,783,190.

HMS *New Zealand* departed Govan on the River Clyde bound for Portsmouth on 19 November 1912. At Portsmouth she was commissioned under the command of Captain Lionel Halsey (RN) on 23 November, being included on the strength of the 1st Cruiser Squadron. At the time of her commissioning three of the ships officers were New Zealanders.

Following working up exercises, sea trials and a visit by King George V, HMS *New Zealand* sailed from Portsmouth on 8 February 1912, bound for New Zealand. This voyage would effectively be a World Cruise with the ship steaming in excess of 50,000 miles and making port visits at St Vincent, Ascension Island, St Helena, Cape town, Durban and Melbourne, Australia before arriving at Wellington, New Zealand on 12 April 1913, to a tumultuous welcome from the People of New Zealand who took great pride in her presence. The Dominions pride in the Capital ship bearing the nations name was echoed in every port she visited on both main Islands. She visited most ports; being either docked or showing herself off the coast in areas that were unsuitable for a ship of her size. She was also shown to the public by standing off the coast of many areas of the Islands that were isolated from the main towns and ports. The ship was present in New Zealand Waters for more than 10 weeks and it was estimated that in excess of 500,000 people visited her during that time.

HMS *New Zealand* departed Auckland Island on 25 June 1913, ultimately bound for the United Kingdom, although she would make many port calls on the way; visiting Suva, Honolulu, Hawaiian Islands, Vancouver, Canada, Panama, Callao and Valparaiso, Chile before continuing South and through the Straits of Magellan and entering the South Atlantic, before turning North and calling at Montevideo, Uruguay and Rio de Janeiro, Brazil, then sailing for the West Indies to visit the main Islands. From here she crossed the North Atlantic Ocean to the United Kingdom, arriving in Home waters around the end of November and docking at Devonport on 8 December 1913. That same month she entered refit following which she joined the 1st Battle Cruiser Squadron of the Home Fleet.

HMS *Australia*. LOC

The third and last *Indefatigable* Class Battlecruiser, HMAS *Australia*, was ordered to be built by John Brown and Company in March 1910, laid down on 26 June 1910 and launched on 25 October 1911. Initially cost was estimated at £2 million, although she was delivered some £295,000 under budget. Following completion she conducted sea trials involving engine runs, gunnery firings and torpedo launchings.

HMAS *Australia* was to form the centerpiece of the RAN (Royal Australian Navy), being the only Capital ship in service with the young naval arm. Captain S. H. Radcliffe, Royal Navy was appointed to command HMAS *Australia* on 17 May 1913, and she was commissioned into the RAN at Portsmouth on 21 June that year. She was designated as Flagship of the RAN, flying the flag of Rear Admiral George Edwin Patey, M.V.O. (later Vice-Admiral K.C.M.G., K.C.V.O.), who had been allocated to command the Australian Fleet on 23 June 1913.

HMAS *Australia* departed Portsmouth in company with the Light Cruiser HMAS *Sydney* on 21 June 1913, bound for Australia, but calling in at Cape Town, South Africa on the way. On Reaching Australia, she sailed for Sydney where she arrived on the morning of 4 October 1913, entering Sydney's Port Jackson port at the head of the Australian Fleet, consisting of the Cruisers HMAS *Melbourne*, *Sydney* and *Encounter* and the Destroyers *Warrego*, *Parramatta* and *Yarra*. HMAS *Australia's* arrival in Sydney was a cause for national pride as it signaled Australia's emergence as an ocean going naval power, which now boasted the most powerful warship of any nation in the Pacific area, including the warships of the European Colonial powers. The Australian Defense Minister at the time, Senator Edward Millen, stated "Since Captain Cook's arrival, no more memorable event has happened than the advent of the Australian Fleet".

The Australian Government and RAN desired to show off their Capital Ship to the nation and HMAS *Australia* embarked upon a tour of Australian ports, calling at Albany, Port Lincoln, Hobart, Glenelg, Melbourne and Townsville in Northern Australia. Her local fame was such that she was the subject of songs and even took a starring role in the movie 'Sea Dogs of Australia', which was released into cinema's on 12 August 1914, eight days after the outbreak of the war between the European Powers on the other side of the world.

HMS *Lion*

The first of the *Lion* Class Battlecruisers, HMS *Lion*, was laid down at Devonport dockyard on 25 November 1909, launched on 6 August 1910 and commissioned on 4 June 1912, under the command of Captain A. A. M. Duff who was appointed in November 1911. She conducted limited steam trials in January 1912, before resuming fitting out, which was completed in May that year. Her build cost was reputed to be £2,083,999. Larger than her predecessors of the *Indefatigable* Class *Lion's* displacement was some 26,250 tons standard and 29,680 tons at full load, and she was the first Battle Cruiser to adopt the 13.5in main gun armament. Her construction had included a spotter's tripod mast aft of the fore-funnel. However, this location saw the mast become vulnerable to interference from smoke and exhaust heat from the funnel. It was, therefore, replaced by a pole mast positioned forward of the fore-funnel in 1912, following the vessels sea trials.

When commissioned on 4 June 1912, *Lion* became Flagship of the 1st Cruiser Squadron of the Hone Fleet, hoisting the flag of Rear-Admiral Lewis Bayly, remaining Flagship when the 1st Cruiser Squadron became the 1st Battle Cruiser Squadron in January 1913. On 1 March 1913, Captain A. E. M. Chatfield took command of her, while at the same time she was allocated as flagship for Rear-Admiral David Beatty, becoming flagship of the fleets Battle Cruiser Squadrons, remaining in this role until the end of the war.

The *Lion* was considered to be a somewhat 'Gloomy' ship in comparison to her sisters *Queen Mary* and *Princess Royal* and in particular compared to HMS *New Zealand*.

HMS Lion (top) was the lead ship of the vessels which became known as the 'Splendid Cats'. These vessels, were faster, heavier armed and armoured than the previous Class's of British Battle Cruiser. HMS Princess Royal was completed more or less to the same standard as the Lion.

HMS *Princess Royal*

Lions sister ship, HMS *Princess Royal*, was laid down at Vickers Yard on 2 May 1910, launched on 24 April (some records suggest 29 April) 1911 and completed in October 1912 at a cost of £2,076,222. *Princess Royal* commissioned at Devonport on 12 November 1912 with Captain O de B Brock (appointed on 1 August 1912) in command. She was allocated to the 1st Cruiser Squadron, remaining with this formation when it changed to the 1st BCS in January 1913.

HMS Queen Mary is listed as the third vessel in the Lion Class, but is actually a Sub- Class, with a number of differences over her half sisters.

HMS *Queen Mary*

Following the two *Lion* Class the Admiralty ordered a modified vessel, which was named HMS *Queen Mary*. This vessel is often described as a separate class from the *Lion* Class – rightly so since the differences are quite considerable in some areas.

HMS *Queen Mary* was a unique vessel being the only one of her type constructed. She was built at a cost of £2,075,491. Ordered to be built at Palmers in the 1910 building program she was laid down on 6 March 1911, launched on 20 March 1912 and commissioned on 4 September 1913, joining the 1st BCS commanded by Captain C. I. Prowse. She was serving with the 1st BCS when war broke out with Germany on 4 August 1914.

HMS Tiger was a single Class vessel, joining the Grand Fleet in late 1914.

HMS *Tiger*

Initially HMS *Tiger* was planned as a fourth unit of the *Lion* Class incorporating the same modifications as the third Unit, HMS *Queen Mary*. However, she was completely redesigned to become the sole vessel of the improved *Tiger* Class as a result of design experience gained in development of the *Kongo* Class Battlecruiser designed by Vickers chief designer Sir George Thurston for the Japanese Navy, the first of which IJN *Kongo* was laid down by Vickers-Armstrong on 17 January 1911. HMS *Tiger* was laid down on 20 June 1912, launched on 15 December 1913 and completed and commissioned in October 1914, at a cost of some £2,100,000.00.

During their respective service careers there were a number of reports that the four 'Cats' known as the 'Splendid Cats' *Lion, Princess Royal and Queen Mary* and *Tiger* attained 30 knots, but it is doubtful that any of them other than the *Tiger* actually managed this speed even for a brief period.

'Speed is armour' was Lord Fishers Maxim. In the new class of warship, which became known as the Battle Cruiser, armour protection was sacrificed for firepower and speed. In contrast, the German Battle Cruisers were more heavily armoured than their British counterparts, achieved at the cost of a knot or two of speed in comparison to their respective British counterparts. Despite this slightly inferior speed of the German vessels, the British Battle Cruisers were never able to overhaul the German vessels before they had reached the safety of their fortified harbours. As an example: with a ship at maximum speed of 24 knots with a 20 mile start over a 28 knot vessel it would take at least five hours to close to within effective gun range of 10 miles, during which a distance of around 130 miles would be covered during a stern chase, which would be typical of the North Sea war. In reality the North Sea simply proved to be too small for such scenarios to result in the successful running down of the German Battle Cruisers before the latter were back in the safety of their fortified anchorages. Thereby, looking back it could be said that the Germans had the major advantage of heavy armour, which saved several vessels from destruction, but the British rarely able to gain from their advantage of superior speed.

In some areas of the pre-war Admiralty, Fisher was regarded as a 'madman' and Winston Churchill was disliked immensely, particularly within the Navy itself; considered to be rude, particularly if criticised. Churchill regarded Fisher as a genius, but a genius who had to be controlled, while Fisher saw Churchill as nothing more than a political figure and treated him as such; fighting him on some issues while supporting him on others. For instance, Fisher had long supported Churchill's selection of Jellico as commander of the Grand Fleet. The appointment of the commander of the 2nd Battle Cruiser Squadron, which was opposed by Beatty, who was not consulted, was supported by both Lord Fisher and Churchill. It was accepted that Fisher and Beatty disliked each other. As early as 1912 it had become clear to observers that Beatty disliked Fisher and vis a vis Fisher disliked Beatty. It is assumed that their mutual dislike was from reputation as when Beatty was favourably mentioned to Fisher in conversation in 1912 he merely replied "Really? Never met him".

While presiding over the Royal Commission on Oil Fuel and Oil, a post he took up on 30 July 1912, Fisher had a vision of Britain's large fleet of warships, particularly the Battle Cruisers, dominating the seas by remaining on station for long periods, refueling at sea when required. His view was that there would be millions of tons of oil fuel always at sea on tankers in transit from port to port. Wireless stations would plot the position of every tanker and all the warships would have to do was intercept them and refuel. While this theory was not realised during the 1914-1918 war, it was a vision of the future and during the Second World War it would be practiced by most of the major naval powers to some degree or other with the United States Navy in particular employing large 'Fleet Trains' to support its drive across the Pacific Ocean.

The Battle Cruiser Squadron was formed in the year immediately prior to the outbreak of war, commanded by Admiral Sir Lewis Bayly who was the first Admiral to command the new squadron, albeit for a short period only. In

February 1913, Vice-Admiral David Beatty was appointed to take over command of the Battle Cruiser Squadron; a considerable honour bestowed upon him by Winston Churchill, being the youngest Admiral on the list. Beatty's flag was hoisted aboard HMS *Lion* on 1 March 1913, while the *Lion* was in dockyard hands.

In spring 1913 Beatty took the BCS to sea for trials, but he had received no formal instructions from the Admiralty on just what he was to train this new fast and powerful arm of the fleet for. Remarkably there was no official naval policy on exactly how the Battle Cruiser Squadron was to be used in war. This was no detriment to Bayly as his period of command of the Battle Cruiser Squadron was very brief, with no time for the formation of such a policy.

In the simplest terms Beatty saw it as **1.** Getting at the enemy; confident that his superior force would allow him to choose the battleground; so to speak. **2.** Destroy the enemy or lead him onto the Battle Fleet to be destroyed. He considered that this should be attempted even at high cost; with no cost being considered too great, even the risk of annihilation of his own force. "If they come out", said Beatty, "I shall consider it my duty to engage them irrespective of odds and I shall possibly lose my squadron".

Ideally Beatty wanted his squadron to manoeuvre and engage the enemy without the requirement for signaling or at least with minimal signaling from the flagship. This ideal was never achieved and of course could be considered as being extremely ambitious and even impracticable.

There were two main functions for the Battlecruisers.
1. Scout ahead of the main Battle Fleet and
2. To act as either bait or a provocation to try and entice the enemy battle fleet (always considered to be the German Fleet) to come out and engage them, thereby drawing them onto the guns of the British Battle Fleet.

In addition 1913 doctrine saw the Battle Cruiser Squadron being used in conjunction with the Light Cruiser Squadrons to conduct reconnaissance of enemy coastlines, support blockading forces or Armoured Cruiser patrols, to act as support between blockading forces and the Battle Fleet when the latter was at sea, and supporting a Cruiser force at sea when tasked to watch an enemy fleet.

Despite being much weaker in armour protection compared with contemporary Battleships of the period the Battlecruisers heavy firepower inevitably meant that an additional role would be to take a place in the line of Battle in a fleet action once the Battle Fleet had become engaged with the enemy. In this role the Battlecruisers would effectively act as a fast division of the Battle Fleet, probably positioned on one of the flanks.

In the first few years, particularly the first six months, of the war the Battlecruisers were used in a varying degree of roles including some that were not in the 1913 doctrine for their planned wartime role. Many of the duties of the Battlecruisers were controversial and were contested by some as they could as effectively have been conducted by smaller vessels or older Battleships.

Pre-war there were informal discussions on prioritising. For operations at high speed and cutting down on what was regarded as dead weight which included torpedo nets and many items and stores normally hauled for long sea voyages, which would not be required for service in the North Sea, although ships would still be required to carry such supplies in the early part of the war.

Towards the end of May 1913 HMS *Lion* was lying in the Cromarty Firth with HMS *Princess Royal, Indefatigable, Indomitable and Invincible*. The Squadron put to sea and during the first days of June 1913 and conducted a series of day and night firing and signaling exercises.

It was at this time that maneuvers were conducted to determine tactics for two large warships of the displacement of a Battlecruiser meeting each other on opposite courses at the high speeds attained by Battlecruisers. *Indomitable* was positioned in the North Sea, about 100 miles or so from the coast. She was to advance towards the coast at high speed. The other Battlecruisers of the Squadron were spread out, with four fifths steam ordered, and tasked to locate and force the *Indomitable* to action. Once *Indomitable's* smoke had been observed on the distant horizon Beatty formed the Battle Cruiser Squadron into line ahead, punching its way through the calm waters of the North Sea towards the *Indomitable*; the ships complements going through the processes of engaging the *Indomitable*, short of course of actually firing. The range and bearing of the *Indomitable* was "telephoned" to the transmitting station to be calculated before the information was sent to the turrets. This was the first time that such an exercise had been conducted, proving invaluable for crews to practice engaging a ship, whose high speed, combined with the high speed of their own vessel, equated to a closing speed of the order of one mile per minute. *Indomitable* had been sighted at a distance of 15 miles and by the time she closed with the Battle Cruiser Squadron 17 minutes had been covered.

Following this important maneuver the Squadron then continued to steam at high speed for 18 hours in a Squadron level engine room test, with *Invincible* proving to the slowest of the Battlecruisers. Although she fell well astern of the *Lion* at the head of the Squadron, she remained visible when the maneuver was concluded. The following morning the Squadron arrived at Portland.

Due to constraints and economies of ammunition, when war broke out in August 1914 the Battle Cruiser Squadron, like the rest of the Battle Fleet, had never fired their main armament guns at anything faster than a target towed at six knots. This led to the unpalatable situation of the Battle Fleet and Battlecruisers entering the war having practiced firing at targets towed at a speed of only six knots or so.

2

THE *GOEBEN* BREAKTHROUGH – AUGUST 1914

In 1912, Britain had withdrawn her big-gun Capital ships from the Mediterranean Fleet in order to concentrate the Battle Fleet in the North Sea, facing the growing threat from the German Fleet. The alliance with France included an understanding that France would be able to deal with any potential threat from the Austria-Hungarian Fleet in the Adriatic and or the Italian Fleet in the Mediterranean and Adriatic. The Royal Navy later dispatched a number of Battlecruisers to join the Mediterranean Fleet to counter the threat from the German Navy *Moltke* Class Battlecruiser SMS *Goeben*, as the French Battleships were too slow to catch her and the British Armoured Cruisers were too slow and also outgunned by the *Goeben*.

In August 1914, the Commander in Chief of the Royal Navy Mediterranean Fleet was Vice Admiral Sir Berkely Milne, flying his flag in the *Invincible* Class Battlecruiser HMS *Inflexible*. *Inflexible* was joined by her sister ship HMS *Indomitable* and the *Indefatigable* Class Battlecruiser HMS *Indefatigable*. The main battery of each of these ships was eight x 12-in guns. The fleet also included the 1st Cruiser Squadron made up of four Armoured Cruisers; the *Duke of Edinburgh* Class Armoured Cruisers HMS *Duke of Edinburgh*, HMS *Black Prince* and HMS *Warrior*, and the *Minotaur* Class Armoured Cruiser HMS *Defence*, under the command of Rear Admiral Troubridge flying his flag in HMS *Warrior*. These were powerful ships, although they were outgunned by the *Goeben* and much slower, with a maximum speed in good condition of only 22-23 knots. The remainder of the 1st Cruiser Squadron was made up of the Light Cruisers HMS *Chatham*, *Weymouth*, *Glasgow* and *Gloucester* with a maximum speed of up to 26+ knots, joined by a flotilla of 12 Destroyers.

On paper none of the British heavy ships could catch the *Goeben*; however, in reality and unknown to the British, the *Goeben* was suffering boiler problems and could only manage a sustained maximum speed of 18-19 knots, which could be increased to 23-24 knots in an emergency for short periods. This meant that not only the British Battlecruisers, but even the old Armoured Cruisers could potentially keep pace with and engage the *Goeben*. This of course was unknown to the British at the time and for some time afterwards.

The French Mediterranean Fleet consisted of six *Danton* Class pre-Dreadnought and one Dreadnought Battleships; with the later flying the flag of the French fleet Commander in Chief. There was also another nine pre-Dreadnought Battleships, 6 Armoured Cruisers and 24 Destroyers, Submarines and a number of smaller warships such as Torpedo Boats. Other ships, including two additional Dreadnought Battleships, joined the French Mediterranean Fleet later, but these were not available on the outbreak of war.

Based at Pola in the Adriatic, the Austrian fleet consisted of three modern Dreadnought and three pre-Dreadnought Battleships supported by a small number of Cruisers and Destroyers. The Italian fleet was geographically closer to the French and British and although Italy had ties with Germany she was fiercely opposed to Austria and seemed unlikely to join in a war alliance with her, although the uncertainty of which side Italy would support or if she would declare neutrality meant that her fleet had to be considered a potential threat. As for Austria, she did not enter the war against Britain until 12 August 1914, by which time the *Goeben* crisis had played itself out.

The SMS Goeben was the only German Capital Ship in the Mediterranean at the outbreak of war in August 1914.

HMS *Indefatigable* was one of 3 Battlecruisers that were at the centre of the British Mediterranean Fleet. This vessel, along with the other elements of the Mediterranean Fleet would be heavily committed to the search for the German warships *Goeben* and *Breslau*.

HMS *Inflexible* visited Constantinople in June 1914 flying Admiral Milne's flag. The Admiral noted that even at that time mines had been laid at the entrance of the Dardanelle's Straits. During the visit H.R.H. the Crown Prince was welcomed aboard the *Inflexible* on a visit. It was noted that during the *Goebens* visit to Constantinople s few months previous, the Crown Prince had not visited the German ship.

Admiral Milne was invited to inspect the Turkish crew which was preparing to depart for Britain crew the new Battleship which had been built in Britain for the Turkish Navy. Of course the coming war would see the new Turkish Battleship requisitioned by the Royal Navy.

Even as the final days of peace counted down to war in late July and the first days of August 1914, the Royal Navy Battlecruisers conducted operations to counter their German opposite numbers, particularly in the Mediterranean, where the British Mediterranean Fleet, including the Battlecruisers HMS

Inflexible (Flagship), HMS *Indomitable* and HMS *Indefatigable* were preparing to shadow and if required engage the German Navy's small Mediterranean force. This small German force consisted of the SMS *Goeben* and the *Magdeburg Class* Light Cruiser SMS *Breslau*. SMS *Goeben* was commanded by Captain Ackermann, and SMS *Breslau* was commanded by Captain Kettner. The German Mediterranean Division also included a detachment of Marines at Skutari, Albania and the Yacht SMS *Loreley,* commanded by Lieutenant-Commander Humman, positioned in the Bosporus. The Light Cruisers SMS *Dresden* and SMS *Strasburg* had been detached to other stations, - the *Dresden* eventually being the only survivor of Von Spee's East Asiatic Cruiser Squadron at the Battle of the Falkland Islands, before eventually being discovered and sunk by HMS *Kent, Glasgow* and *Orama* off the Chilean Pacific coast on 14 March 1915.

The Light Cruiser *Breslau* was armed with a battery of 12 x 4.1-in guns and had a maximum speed of 27 knots. In fully working condition the *Goeben* was a formidable warship, capable of 29 knots and armed with a main battery of ten 11.-in guns. Although these weapons were slightly lower in striking power to the British 12-in guns arming the Royal Navy Battlecruisers in the Mediterranean, *Goeben* technically outgunned any single Battlecruiser of the *Invincible* or *Indefatigable* Class as she had ten large caliber guns to the British ships eight. She was also heavier than the British ships at 23,000 tons, with a much heavier and more complete armour protection suite compared to the British Battlecruisers. It was generally accepted that one for one she was superior to the British ships of the *Invincible* or *Indefatigable* Class. However, in summer 1914 the *Goeben* was suffering a number of problems. She was plagued by leaky boilers, which considerably reduced her maximum speed and her range. For this reason among others the German Navy had planned to replace the *Goeben* in the Mediterranean Division with her sister ship SMS *Moltke* at Algeciras on 4 October 1914. These plans were abandoned as the international crisis worsened in the last days of July 1914. In the event of war between the Anglo-French alliance and Germany, the German Mediterranean Divisions position would be untenable as she was faced with overwhelming superiority in numbers of warships.

In the Month preceding the outbreak of war HMS *Indefatigable* along with other British warships had conducted a Mediterranean cruise, making a number of port calls, including Phalerum Bay (Athens), Marmarice, Larnaka, Alexandretta and Beirut. This cruise was completed towards the end of July 1914, following which *Indefatigable* was to return to Malta, conducting exercises with other fleet units during the passage. The ships company's were informed of the deteriorating international situation by-telegram on 24 July 1914.

On 27 July 1914, Admiral Milne received a telegram, described as "the preliminary telegram of warning" that the international situation was worsening by the hour and that war was a possibility. At this time most of the British Mediterranean Fleet was at Alexandria, Egypt with the force consisting of HMS

Inflexible (Flagship), HMS *Indefatigable*, the Armoured Cruisers HMS *Warrior* and *Black Prince*, four Light Cruisers and 13 Destroyers. At this time the Armoured Cruiser HMS *Defence* (flying the flag of Rear-Admiral Troubridge) and the Destroyer HMS *Grampus* were at Durazzo in the Adriatic as was the German Light Cruiser Breslau and the French Cruiser Edgar Quinet. All these nations' ships were present to support the International conference taking place at Scutari. This conference was aimed at finding a solution to the future of Albania. As noted later the British Light Cruiser HMS *Gloucester* was apparently also at Durazzo

Following receipt of the warning telegram on 27 July, Admiral Milne telegrammed the Admiral Superintendant at Malta to instruct that all measures be taken to defend against any possible attack and a message was sent to Rear-Admiral Troubridge in HMS *Defence* at Durazzo to the necessary precautions against being attacked.

On 27 July *Indomitable* was preparing to enter refit at Malta and HMS *Duke of Edinburgh* had just completed her refit.

The British Mediterranean Fleet departed Alexandria on 28 July, bound for Malt. The planned exercises had been cancelled as the fleet to made preparations for war during the passage. At 5.10 p.m. on the 28th, a telegram was received notifying the fleet that Austria had declared war on Serbia making the likelihood of war between France and Germany far greater, with the increasing possibility of Britain joining in the war against Germany.

The Squadron consisted of HMS *Inflexible* (Flagship), HMS *Indefatigable* and the Armoured Cruisers HMS *Warrior* and *Black Prince* (located 0.5 miles on the port beam) and four Light Cruisers HMS *Chatham, Dublin, Gloucester* and *Weymouth*, which, were spread out ahead of the Squadron's heavy units, with twelve Destroyers some 2 miles on the starboard beam.

Initially the Squadrons speed was leisurely, but this was later increased to 17 knots and then again twice on the 29th, until speed was 20 knots, resulting in HMS *Warrior* dropping behind. On the morning of 30 July, HMS *Defence* and other ships joined the squadron, having sailed from Durazzo, with the entire squadron arriving at Malta at 11.00 am that morning (some records indicate that the Squadron arrived at Malta on the 29th).

Also at Malta was the Battlecruiser HMS *Indomitable*, which had only just entered-refit, but capable of joining the Squadron at short notice. *Indomitable* had weighed from Beirut on 21 July 1914, bound for Malta for her scheduled refit, arriving there on 24 July and entering refit on the 28th.

On 30 July 1914, Winston Churchill, following a discussion with the First Sea Lord regarding Mediterranean War Orders (dated 1913), signaled the C in C (Commander in Chief) Mediterranean Fleet informing him that war with Germany seemed probable and the expectation that Italy would declare neutrality. The signal continued "Your first task should be to aid the French in the transportation of their African Army by covering and if possible bringing to action individual fast German ships, particularly *Goeben*, which may interfere with that transportation. You will be notified by telegram when you may consult with the French Admiral. Except in combination with the French as part of a general battle, do not at this stage be brought to action against superior forces. You must husband your resources and we shall hope to reinforce the Mediterranean". Churchill had vastly overestimated the power of the two German warships, and quite distinct from requesting British assistance to help protect their troop convoys, by 6 August the French were offering to attach six Armoured Cruisers to the British force tasked with finding the *Goeben*. What seems clear from the signal is the appreciation that the *Goeben* was on paper superior to any one of the three British Battlecruisers then in the Mediterranean Fleet and that the C in C should keep at least two if not three of them in close company to ensure overwhelming fire power against the *Goeben*.

According to Admiral Milne's writings, the fleet was ready for operational service by the afternoon of 1 August 1914.

On 2 August, the C in C received another signal, "*Goeben* must be shadowed by two battle cruisers. Approaches to Adriatic must be watched by cruisers and destroyers. Remain near Malta yourself. It is believed that Italy will remain neutral but you cannot absolutely rely on that". This certainly confirmed that the Admiralty wanted a concentration of at least two British Battlecruisers in any confrontation with the *Goeben*. It also took away much of the potential scope for initiative on the part of the C in C, with orders on how to conduct his operation coming from offices in London, which lacked any first-hand knowledge of the situation on the ground (sea). By ordering the Commander in Chief to remain near Malta while he was flying his flag in the Battlecruiser HMS *Inflexible* meant that one Battlecruiser was effectively out of the wider search for the *Goeben*, reducing the British to only two in the event of the *Goeben* being discovered outside the vicinity of Malta. More importantly they were effectively handicapping the C in C's ability to conduct operations against the German warships by taking away his ability to decide upon the movements of his warships himself, or indeed the movements of his Flagship, which would not be present at any action unless the *Goeben* could be brought to action close to Malta.

On arrival at Malta, *Inflexible, Indefatigable* and other elements of the Squadron took on coal and stores including replenishing ammunition stocks during 31 July and 1 August. At the same time, the Malta Harbour defenses were prepared and manned as war clouds gathered on the horizon. On 1 August, intelligence reports indicated that the *Goeben* was in port in Brindisi around 50 miles inside the entrance to the Adriatic Sea. However, this information was inaccurate, with Goeben actually being en-route from Pola to Messina on 1 August, arriving at Messina on the 2nd.

Admiral Wilhelm Souchon had taken over as commander of the German Mediterranean Division on 23 October 1913, flying his Flag in SMS *Goeben* at Trieste. During the remaining ten months of peace *Goeben* visited many ports and conducted a number of cruises. Following the news of the assassination of Arch Duke Ferdinand, Admiral Souchon began to prepare for the possibility of hostilities between Germany and one or more of the nations of the Triple Entente of France, Russia and Great Britain, with the first priority to try and get the leaky boilers tubes replaced.

Souchon issued a request to the German secretary of state to dispatch boiler tubes and work crews to the Austrian port of Pola in the Adriatic Sea, where the *Goeben* was to sail for, with the plan to reach the port a few days in advance of the new tubes and work party. Once at Pola, work on getting the *Goeben* as fit for war service as possible commenced as fast as the crew could be driven in the July Mediterranean heat, with work being conducted in day and night shifts. Although most of the damaged tubes were replaced, there remained a number of problems prohibiting *Goeben* from attaining anything close to her maximum speed. She sailed from Pola after 13 days in port and reached Messina, near the North East tip of Sicily, across the straits from the toe of Italy, on 2 August. During the journey she had to shut off a number of boilers resulting in the inevitable loss of steam reducing speed to only 18 knots, although this could be extended to 24 knots for a short period in an emergency.

In early July, the Light Cruiser SMS *Breslau* was anchored off the coast of Durazzo, Albania in the Adriatic along with a number of warships of other nations supporting the local government. The British Light Cruiser HMS *Gloucester*, which would soon be involved in the hunt for the German warships, was also lying off Durazzo and the crews of *Breslau* and *Gloucester* were on friendly terms during the stay, apparently participating in a daily game of water polo. Souchon informed the *Breslau* of the international situation on 8 July, and once German mobilization had been announced he recalled her from Durazzo, although she was apparently the last of the international gathering of warships to leave.

Admiral Milne received news on Sunday 2 August that the day previous the *Goeben* had been at Brindisi, but unknown to the British command the *Goeben* had simply rendezvoused with the *Breslau* near Brindisi before proceeding on to Messina to coal. At 2.00 p.m. on the afternoon of 2 August, the Squadron consisting of the Battlecruisers HMS *Indomitable,* and *Indefatigable,* the 1st Cruiser Squadron and Destroyers of the 1st and 2nd Divisions, received a signal ordering them to raise steam and prepare to put to sea that evening. The Flagship HMS *Inflexible* and a number of destroyers were to remain at Malta, while *Indefatigable and Indomitable* were to sail with the Squadron under the command of the Rear Admiral 1st Cruiser Squadron flying his Flag in the Armoured Cruiser HMS *Defence*, with the Armoured Cruisers HMS *Duke of Edinburgh* and *Warrior*, the Light Cruisers HMS *Chatham, Gloucester* and *Weymouth* and Destroyers of the 1st and 2nd Divisions. The Armoured Cruiser HMS *Black Prince* had detached from the Squadron on the afternoon of 2 August, bound for Durazzo to pick up the military details that had been left there and return them to Malta. HMS *Indomitable* signaled that she would not be ready for sea until around 8.00 pm as she had emptied her bunkers and the ships magazines as part of her refit preparation and she would, therefore, have to coal and re-stock her magazines.

At 9.00 pm on 2 August, *Indefatigable, Indomitable, Defence* (Flagship), *Duke of Edinburgh, Warrior Chatham Gloucester and Weymouth,* along with the 1st and 2nd Divisions of Destroyers, weighed from Malta and proceeded North-Eastward on course N. 56 degrees E, at speeds of between 15 and 17 knots. This hastily prepared naval force was tasked with watching the approaches to the Adriatic Sea. The two Battlecruisers, *Indomitable* and *Indefatigable* were tasked with monitoring close to the entrance to the Adriatic during daylight hours, before retiring southward before darkness fell when the Light Cruisers and Destroyers would take over during the hours of darkness, before returning to replenish coal stocks during daylight hours. The object of the operation was basically to try to detect and shadow the *Goeben* and *Breslau*, as tensions with Germany were reaching a crescendo. Although Britain and Germany were not at war it was expected that the *Goeben* and *Breslau* would put to sea amid the rising international tensions. With the possibility of war breaking out between the nations at any time it was desirable for the Royal Navy to know the whereabouts of the German warships, particularly if they entered the Mediterranean Sea.

One dilemma facing the British Commanders was that the German vessels had a slight speed advantage of around 2 to 3 knots over the British Battlecruisers, which could make it difficult for the *Indomitable* and *Indefatigable* to stay in contact with the German ships, assuming they were detected. The Royal Navy command was at this time unaware that the *Goeben* was experiencing boiler problems, which had significantly reduced her attainable maximum speed.

At 11.35 pm on 2 August the British force received a signal from the Commander in Chief, "Situation very critical, be prepared to meet surprise attack, concentrate your force while on passage, recall Destroyers to join you". At this time the British still thought that the *Goeben* was at Brindisi, but within hours became aware that she was actually at Messina. The British Battlecruisers received this news at 05.45 am on 3 August, when they were informed that the Light Cruiser HMS *Chatham* had been ordered to pass through the Straits of Messina and report any movements by the German ships, particularly if they steamed on a northerly course. At 10.10 am HMS *Indomitable* signaled *HMS Indefatigable* "If we are detached and coming into battle with enemy, I hope you will haul out of line sufficiently if we are in that formation, to use your guns without signal from me. To save coal keep just out of our wake as a rule, only getting into it when we are turning". This signal seemed in effect to give *Indefatigable* a free hand to engage the *Goeben* at the earliest opportunity without waiting for orders from *Indomitable* in the event contact was made. Of course, at this time Britain and Germany were not yet at war.

Having been detached since 3.15 pm on the 3rd, the Commander in Chief in HMS *Inflexible* signaled *Indomitable*, *Indefatigable* and *Chatham* at 5.00 pm while some 20 miles from Malta, "After meeting search for *Goeben* at 14 knots between Cape Bon and Cape Spartivento as far as 40 degrees N., 13 degrees 0 E., shadow *Goeben* if found. Ships not to separate too far. Guard against surprises, light fires in all boilers". While the Battlecruisers had been ordered to proceed westward in search of the *Goeben*, the Armoured Cruisers HMS *Defence* and *Black Prince* steamed to lend support to the Destroyers patrolling the area of the Straits of Otranto in the Ionian Islands.

As night approached the ships were darkened at 7.35 pm and at 8.47 pm *Indomitable* received signal "Raise steam 22 knots. Chase, present course. Show no lights at all". Another signal received by *Indomitable* and *Indefatigable* from the Commander in Chief around 10.30 pm read "Proceed to Gibraltar at 22 knots in readiness to prevent *Goeben* leaving Mediterranean. *Chatham* rejoining Flag 36 degrees 23' N., 14 degrees 41' E. by 6 am Tuesday (4 August) at 20 knots. I am using oil as requisite". With HMS *Chatham* ordered to leave the Battlecruisers and return to Malta, *Indomitable* sent a signal to *Indefatigable* at 10.44 pm reading "When we pass Pantellaria we will burn navigation lights and show a few other lights and if possible pass as merchant ships and show ourselves to Defence Mobile clearly". The hope was that there were German spies, or at least spies of other nationalities sympathetic to Germany in Pantellaria who would pass information by cable to Vittoria in Sicily where it would then be passed by Wireless/Transmitter (W/T) to the *Goeben*. The *Goeben*, it was hoped would then come out to attack the merchant ships, which actually being the British Battlecruisers, could then be brought to action.

While the British were facing the problems of locating the German Warships, the Germans were not short on problems themselves. When the *Goeben* and *Breslau* arrived at Messina they found that the Italians, far from supporting the German position, refused to issue coal or supplies to the German warships. To try and counter the problem of lack of fuel Souchon ordered a number of German Merchant steamers to come alongside the *Goeben* in order to coal her from their bunkers. Souchon had recalled the steamer ss *General* out of Hamburg and it arrived at Messina with the *Goeben*. The passengers were ordered off the ship and given money for their transport fares and the ship was duly requisitioned by Souchon to act as a supply ship for his two-ship squadron. The *General* took on reserve stocks and other supplies as well as some fittings removed from the *Goeben* and would follow behind the German warships to their destination under the command of Captain Fiedler.

At Messina Souchon drew up a plan of action, which was to proceed to the Algerian coast and conduct a bombardment of the embarkation ports used by the French XIX Army Corp as well as the coastal forts of Bona and

Philippeville. His plan was for the *Goeben* and *Breslau* to be off the Algerian coast at daybreak on the morning of 4 August, Therefore, his ships quietly left Messina under cover of darkness at 01.00 am on the 4th. By now Souchon had been informed that Germany and France were at war, the information being received not long before the ships departed Messina. When still some two hours from the planned bombardment time, the *Goeben* received a signal bearing an order from the Kaiser for the ships to proceed to the Turkish port at Constantinople "forthwith." However, as dawn approached the German ships proceeded on their course for the Algerian Coast. Souchon had decided to continue with the planned bombardment before carrying out the Kaisers order. At dawn the shells from the *Goebens* 11-in guns fell around the port facilities and transports at Bona and Philippeville giving the *Goeben* the distinction of being the first capital ship to fire a shot in anger during World War 1.

Due to a lack of decent coal, Souchen opted not to take the direct route to the Dardanelles and instead decided to go via the Straits of Messina, hoping to find German or other friendly steamers to coal from. In the hours immediately following the bombardment the German warships put as much distance between themselves and the Algerian Coast as possible, hoping to reach Messina without being discovered.

At just after 06.00 am on the 4th, the British Commander in Chief in HMS *Inflexible* was in a position N., 38 degrees E., some 24 miles from Valletta, Malta, in company with a force of Torpedo Boat Destroyers, while HMS *Hussar* and *Weymouth* were positioned between Valletta and Cape Correnti, Italy. At 09.35 am GMT, while the command decision on whether the *Indomitable* and *Indefatigable* should head for Gibraltar at full speed or continue steaming west at 22 knots while they awaited further instructions from the Commander in Chief, was being pondered, the German Light Cruiser *Breslau* was spotted about 2 points on the starboard bow of HMS *Indomitable*. At this time the British Battlecruisers were steering course N. 84.5 degrees W. with the German ship on a N.E. by E., course at what appeared to the British to be a high speed, estimated at in excess of 22 knots, producing a large bow wave as she punched through the Mediterranean Sea. Within moments the *Goeben* came into view on the port bow, but slightly to starboard in comparison to *Breslau*, on a course which appeared to be E. by N., again at high speed. (It should be remembered that it is now known the *Goeben* was restricted in her maximum attainable speed to around 23 knots or under and that only for short periods.)

According to the British version of events, on spotting the British Battlecruisers the *Goeben* altered course on a heading which would appear to have been intending to cross ahead of the British ships and join up with the *Breslau*. The British Battlecruisers then altered course to starboard, followed by the *Goeben* altering course again to resume her original course. When the *Breslau* had been sighted the British ships sounded action stations, although the guns were ordered to remain trained in the securing positions. It should be remembered that Britain and Germany were not at war at this time. Lookouts were ordered to report if *Goeben* was flying an Admirals Flag and to keep watch on her guns to see if they were being trained on the British ships. Range was initially 17,000 to 19,000 yards, but as the range closed it was reported that the *Goebens* guns remained trained fore and aft in the securing position. It was claimed in post accounts that the search for an Admiral's flag was ordered so that if one was detected the British ships could fire a salute from the saluting guns, which they hoped would be mistaken for the British firing on the German ships. However, it was reported that no Admirals Flag could be observed. The British and German warships passed each other going in opposite directions with the *Breslau* passing to starboard and the *Goeben* passing to port of the British ships at a speed estimated by the British to be in the region of 20 knots.

An account originating from HMS *Indefatigable* gives the time on meeting *Breslau* and *Goeben* as around 10.30 am, although this can be safely discounted as being a mistake. This same account gave the estimated speed of the *Goeben* as about 15 knots, with *Goeben* being passed at about 8,000 yards. The British ships then turned to port in order to follow *Goeben*, but maneuvering to remain outside of direct line of her wake during shadowing.

According to Souchons notes, at 10.00 am on 4 August he sighted a pair of large warships on his port bow while steaming in the opposite direction to the German ships at a very high speed. The German ships went to action station but kept their course and as the range decreased the distinctive shape of the tripod masts of the British Battlecruisers became apparent, confirming that the ships were British and not French. The two British Battlecruisers were observed to pass the German ships at a range of around 10,000 yards before turning to follow them. The shadowing had begun if not the hunt. The British and Germans were still not at war, therefore, neither side opened fire on the other, although in his writings Souchon claimed that although he had not been informed of war between Britain and Germany, he wondered why the British had not opened fire on his ships as it was his observation that "England has invariably commenced war by attacking her foes before any declaration of war". By England he obviously meant Britain, and throughout history would not be the last person to wrongly label Great Britain as England. It continues to happen even in the 21st Century.

Although, the many reports gave varying times for the initial sightings it can be assumed that a short time after 09.30 am is the more accurate due to the timings of a number of signals. At 09.40 am (GMT) a signal was sent to the Commander in Chief reading, "Enemy in sight 37 degrees 44' N., 7 degrees 56' E., steering east, consisting of *Goeben* and *Breslau*". *Indomitable* then signaled *Indefatigable* "Raise steam for full speed. I am going to shadow her". As the British Battlecruisers turned to get in behind the *Goeben*, the *Breslau* appeared to increase speed and headed north and by 11.30 am she was out of sight of the British warships.

With the British ships now obviously shadowing the German warships as well as attempting to jam their wireless communications, the German commander knew he must try to shake of the shadows. Although not at war with Britain, he was aware that war with Britain was possible if not expected, and in any case, the British would possibly be passing the movements of the German ships on to the French. Souchon therefore ordered the *Goebens* speed to be increased to its maximum of 23 knots, available for short periods due to the ongoing boiler problems.

At 10.15 am (GMT) the Commander in Chief back near Malta in *Inflexible* had sent W/T signal "Shadow *Goeben*". Another signal informed that the Light Cruiser HMS *Dublin* had been dispatched from the region of Biserta (also known as Bizerta) with orders to support *Indomitable* and *Indefatigable*, and the Light Cruiser HMS *Chatham* apparently was to proceed to Biserta.

At 11.20 am *Indomitable* signaled *Indefatigable* "Chase *Goeben* and keep her in sight", followed by a further signal later asking "Do you think we (*Indefatigable* and *Indomitable*) are close enough to her? (*Goeben*)"; with "Yes, just about", being signaled back to *Indomitable* from *Indefatigable* in reply. This prompted a further signal from *Indomitable* to *Indefatigable*, "If it gets thicker we will have to go one on each quarter and closer". This signal was in response to the weather, which as the morning wore on into the afternoon became hazy, sometimes causing the *Goeben* to be obscured from view from the British ships, even when the range was closed down to 6,500 yards, within the torpedo range of the German vessels. Although this was a concern it was the only way the *Goeben* could be kept in sight in the haze. Range was also reduced at times due to frequent alterations in speed by the *Goeben*, which at one time caused the British Battlecruisers to have to reduce speed by as much as 8 knots in order to keep a reasonable distance between themselves and the German vessel.

After the *Goeben* had closed up with the *Breslau* again around 1.20 pm Indomitable signaled to *Indefatigable* "Do not steer in their wake". By this time the German ships were following a zigzag course and it was feared that they could drop mines in the path of the British ships. By 2.00 pm the Light Cruiser HMS *Dublin* had came into sight on the British Battlecruisers starboard bow and a W/T message intended for the Commander in Chief, back at Malta in HMS *Inflexible*, was intercepted. This read "War imminent, send Destroyer flotilla as fast as coal permits. Keep well clear of Italian coast, retaining *Gloucester* (a Light Cruiser) to watch Adriatic". In mid-afternoon *Indomitable* ordered the *Dublin* "to keep to starboard side of ships ahead out of range".

An account from HMS *Indefatigable* gives her speed after 3.00 pm as 23 knots, and *Indomitable* about 20-21 knots, with *Goeben*, *Breslau* and HMS *Dublin* about 27 knots, although as stated before, the *Goeben* was apparently capable of only 23-24 knots for short periods only and around 19 knots sustained.

At 3.48 pm (unclear if local or GMT) *Indefatigable* received a message from *Indomitable* ordering her to "increase speed and take position off port quarter of

Goeben, so as to prevent her escaping to port if possible without being seen by one of us (British ships)". This was part of the plan to position the *Dublin* to starboard, *Indefatigable* on port quarter (beam) of the *Goeben* while the *Indomitable* remained astern of the German ships before the haze became too murky and or night closed in. By this time the haze on the eastern horizon was thickening and sometimes forming in thick banks. Within a minute *Indefatigable* received a further message from *Indomitable* ordering her to "chase; keep in sight of Germans. Use oil fuel as requisite".

Around 4.00 pm it was noted that the Germans were pulling away and *Indomitable* ordered speed to be increased to as fast as the engineers could provide and sent a W/T signal to the Commander in Chief reading "Germans running away from us, steering E. 26 or 27 knots…" Obviously the German speed had been miss-calculated as was previously seen the *Goeben* was barely capable of 24 knots even for short periods. *Indomitable* noted that from around 4.00 pm (local; 3.00 pm GMT) *Dublin* reported that the two German ships continually separated before re-forming again at all times keeping on course E. or E. by N. This continued apparently until *Dublin* lost sight of them. At 4.00 pm, *Dublin* had signaled to the Commander in Chief near Malta in *Inflexible*, also picked up by *Indomitable*, "*Breslau* parting company from *Goeben*, shall I engage her?" to which she received a very quick reply from *Indomitable* reading "No, do not let them get between you and me". A short time later the *Dublin* received a signal from the Commander in Chief also refusing permission to engage the *Breslau*. (Again, it should be remembered that Britain and Germany were still not yet at war.) At this time the *Indomitable* was punching through the sea at 22 knots, which was as fast as she could make, on course N. 85 degrees., E., This slower speed was later claimed to be due to the lack of 90 stockers for her boiler rooms and the fact that she was overdue a refit. *Indefatigable* was positioned between one and two miles on the *Indomitable* port bow, while the *Dublin* was positioned between 1 and 1.5 points on *Indomitable*'s starboard bow, about 12-16,000 yards ahead. The Germans remained to the fore of *Indomitable;* still in sight physically, or when not their smoke remaining in sight. Just after 4.00 pm (local) the *Dublin* signaled *Indomitable* that the German "Cruisers have separated, *Goeben* to N.W. apparently, *Breslau* to S.E".

By 7.00 pm *Dublin* was only just able to keep *Goeben* in sight. By this time the British Battlecruisers were about 80 miles from Cape Bon in the area between westward of Sicily and to the south of Sardinia with the *Goeben* around 30 miles further east. Eventually HMS *Dublin* was ordered to continue shadowing *Goeben*, at least until darkness fell, while the British Battlecruisers were ordered onto a westward course, reducing speed at the same time.

The German account states that the two British Battlecruisers began to lag behind slightly as the afternoon wore on, and aided by a mist that appeared before nightfall, the Germans lost sight of the last British ship at 9.00 pm on 4 August, appearing to have shaken of their unwanted shadows.

At 02.00 am on the 5th, *Indefatigable* and *Indomitable* received the message that as Britain's ultimatum to Germany regarding the latter's attack on Belgium had expired at 01.00 GMT; hostilities were to be commenced against Germany. Following this *Indefatigable, Indomitable* and their supporting Light Cruisers were ordered to steam to an area off Pantelleria Island, in the Sicily Straits, where they would join HM*S Inflexible* with the Commander in Chief.

It was not until the morning of 5 August that the German ships crews found out that Britain had declared war on Germany on 4 August. By this time the *Goeben* and *Breslau* had proceeded along the Sicilian coast during the night of 4 August and the early hours of 5 August, during which time they encountered a Destroyer Flotilla in the darkness, but due to the brightness of the moon were able to identify them as being Italian. Arriving back at Messina on the 5th, the crews of the *Goeben* and *Breslau* immediately set about coaling as much as they could and preparing the ships for sea again as it was desired to leave again as quickly as possible. Souchon sent a signal to Austro-Hungarian Admiral Haus requesting that he send the Austro-Hungarian Fleet to the assistance of the German ships. He received reply signal effectively bearing excuses that he was unable to come out, and then that to attempt to rescue the German ships from the blockading Anglo-French navies was "hopeless", and it would not be attempted.

At Messina, about 400 volunteers from many of the ships in harbour and elsewhere had been selected from many more wanting to join the German ships; brining the ships up to their war complements. Some of the Volunteers were claimed by Souchon to be American. This is a subject which appears to have been ignored throughout the intervening period of 97 years. Although the American position on the war in the early months certainly did not favour Great Britain and as a nation she gave much material and propaganda support to Germany in her fight against Britain. Of course, it should also be remembered that Great Britain was considered the United States of America's natural enemy at the time; therefore, it would seem logical that Germany would receive sympathy and support from America in her fight against the British Empire.

Before sailing from Messina Souchon was informed by a German Admiralty signal that "Entering Constantinople temporarily impossible owing to political consideration". He was then advised by the German Naval Attaché in Rome to sail for the Adriatic and join the Austro-Hungarian Fleet there. However, in his writings Souchon states that he did not enter the Adriatic as by joining the Austro-Hungarian Fleet he would be "condemned to inactivity". As his position in the Mediterranean was untenable, he decided to sail for the Dardanelles with the aim of entering the Bosporus and on to the Black Sea, even if it meant entering the Dardanelles without Turkish consent. The one ace Souchon held was that the British did not know what his destination would be, and history would show that sailing for the Dardanelles was something that was not really considered within British circles. The clear weather and moonlit nights would give him some protection against Destroyer attacks, and so long as he could avoid being dragged into a slugging match with the British Battlecruisers the Germans thought they had a good chance of reaching their destination.

To reach Constantinople Souchon arranged by wireless for a steamer carrying 800 tons of coal to de sent to a point south of Cape Maleas, Greece, with another to come out from Constantinople to the area of the most southern Cyclades Island. At Messina the Germans took on coal from whatever source they could and Souchon claims that they even received some coal from a British steamer. The Governor at Messina sent a note urging the Germans to remain in the port longer than 24 hours and Souchon informed him that he would be gone within that time even though 72 hours was the time limit under international law. It was Souchons initial plan to delay departure until 5.00 pm on 6 August to give him a better chance of escaping the British warships he knew would be searching for him. However, the Goeben and *Breslau* weighed and departed Messina at 12.00 pm on the afternoon of 6 August. The German commander had been informed that both exits of the Straits of Messina were being watched by British warships, and a British Cruiser had apparently been sighted by the *Goeben* cruising off the southern approaches to Messina. He had been informed through a consular agent in Milazzo, Sicily, that a force of large British warships was stationed close to the northern entrance to the Straits near the Lipari Islands. This information had apparently originated with Italian Coast artillery units, which claimed to have observed the ships.

The German ships sailed through the southern entrance to the Straits where the Light Cruiser HMS *Gloucester* was waiting. The clear night and calm sea aided *Gloucester* in keeping the Germans within visual range and allowed her to continue shadowing when the German ships altered course to starboard. *Goeben* attempted to interfere with *Gloucester's* wireless communications, but this was only attempted intermittently for periods of an hour or so.

The German records show *Gloucester* shadowing the *Goeben* and *Breslau* until 12.00 pm on the afternoon of 7 August, following which there was an exchange of fire between *Gloucester* and *Breslau,* then *Goeben* joined *Breslau* in engaging *Gloucester,* which being hopelessly outgunned was forced to retire. During the engagement the *Breslau* was hit by a single shell on the ships side, but this did no serious damage. The Germans could not believe their luck. Despite steaming at a speed of only 18 knots due to *Goebens* boiler difficulties, no other British Cruisers, Battlecruisers or even Destroyers had appeared, allowing the German ships to steam into the Aegean Sea at which point they split up. *Goeben* headed for a pre-positioned collier, which she was to rendezvous with on 8 August, staying clear of land as it waited for coal. As *Goeben* could not attain direct communications with Constantinople, the steamer *General* had been dispatched to Smyrna where she could communicate with Constantinople for the *Goeben*. She forwarded a message from *Goeben* reading "Do your utmost to enable me to enter the Straits, with the permission of the Turkish Government, if necessary without their formal sanction". After daylight came on 9 August, *Goeben*, followed a short time later by the *Breslau* and then in the afternoon by the German collier *Bogador* (*Bogador* had disguised herself as the Greek steamer *Plymitis*) stopped and anchored in the bay of the small Island of Denusa. When the steamer arrived *Goeben* began to coal, continuing through the night, before departing for the Dardanelles at dawn. The ship was at action stations as they feared a British Squadron could be waiting for them at the entrance to the Dardanelles.

It was also feared that they may have to try to force their way in by engaging the Dardanelles forts, something the Germans appear to think they could have done, although history would show that even a large force of capital ships, some much more powerful than he *Goeben*, would have extreme difficulty in forcing its way up the heavily defended Dardanelles. That said, in August 1941 the Dardanelles defences were much less formidable than they would become several months later.

Goeben passed the Island of Tenedos in the Northern Adriatic at 4.00 pm and then headed for the entrance to the straits, hoping they would not have to fight. *Goeben* signaled a Turkish station at Cape Helles requesting that they send a Pilot out to take them in and then a Turkish Gunboat-Torpedo Boat appeared at the entrance to the Straits and signaled, "Follow me". The *Goeben* and *Breslau* had escaped interception and destruction by the British and as dusk was approaching the ships anchored near Chanak with lookouts claiming to have sighted a foreign warship outside the entrance to the Straits.

There was much criticism of Admiral Milne's failure to bring the Goeben to action and destroy her. On 30 August 1914, a statement was issued by the Admiralty stating that "The conduct and dispositions of Admiral Sir Berkeley Milne in regard to the German vessels Goeben and Breslau has been the subject of the careful examination of the Board of Admiralty, with the result that their Lordships have approved the measures taken by him in all respects".

Note: The Austro-Hungarian Fleet included three Dreadnought and three pre-Dreadnought Battleships, while the Italians, which it was considered highly possible would ally herself with German had three Dreadnought and four pre-Dreadnought Battleships. On paper therefore, the 15 Anglo-French capital ships outnumbered the 14 of the Central Powers and Italy. However, the Central Powers and Italy had six modern Dreadnought Battleships and a modern Battlecruiser compared to the single Dreadnought of France and the three Battlecruisers of the British Mediterranean Fleet. These Battlecruisers, however, while powerfully armed, were much lighter armoured than modern Dreadnought Battleships and would have been highly vulnerable against Battleships, particularly if they accepted battle with the combined Dreadnoughts of Austria-Hungary and Italy. Even the Battle Fleets of either Austria-Hungary or Italy could have in all probability overpowered the British Battlecruisers.

British Mediterranean Fleet at the outbreak of War – 4 August 1914

Commanded by Admiral Sir A. Berkeley Milne, Bt., G.C.V.O K.C.B

2nd Battle Cruiser Squadron
HMS *Inflexible (Captain Arthur N. Loxley; Admiral Milne's Flagship)*,
HMS *Indomitable (Captain Charles F. Sowerby)*
HMS *Indefatigable (Captain Francis W. Kennedy)*

1st Cruiser Squadron - Armoured Cruisers

HMS *Warrior*
HMS *Black Prince*
HMS *Duke of Edinburgh*
HMS *Defence*

Light Cruisers

HMS *Chatham*
HMS *Dublin*
HMS *Glasgow*
HMS *Gloucester*
HMS *Weymouth*
(Admiral Milne's account states only four Light Cruisers under his command)

Destroyers 1st and 2nd Divisions – 12 Destroyers

German Mediterranean Squadron and Ancillary vessels

Battlecruiser SMS *Goeben*
Light Cruiser SMS *Breslau*
Merchant vessel *General*

3

HMAS *AUSTRALIA* IN THE PACIFIC - AUGUST 1914 TO JANUARY 1915

When war with Germany broke out Australia took her place with the United Kingdom, and her fleet, including the *Indefatigable* Class Battle Cruiser HMAS *Australia*, took were placed under Admiralty control, and the ship, along with other RAN (Royal Australian Navy) units, immediately took up the role of hunting the German East Asiatic Cruiser Squadron under the command of Admiral Maximilian Graf Von Spee. With the 12-in guns of HMAS *Australia* being vastly superior to anything in the German Cruiser squadron, the Better part of valour seemed appropriate and Von Spee took the squadron to South America's Pacific coast with the aim of entering into the South Atlantic via the Cape as he was unable to return to his base at Tsingtao, Eastern China, which was invested by Japanese and British forces. The powerful Japanese fleet was hunting him in this area, along with some British ships, including the *Swiftsure* Class Pre-Dreadnought Battleship HMS *Triumph*.

On 4 August 1914 HMAS *Australia* sailed from Sydney on a northward heading and joined up with the *Chatham* Class Light Cruiser HMAS *Sydney* and three Destroyers, *Parramatta, Warrego* and *Yarra,* south of New Guinea on the 9th. This powerful force then proceeded to Rabaul on the Island of New Britain, which was a major German base and administration hub for the German forces in the Pacific. On the evening of 11 August, the Australian ships took up station off Rabaul where it was thought that the German Pacific cruiser squadron might be anchored. While HMAS *Australia* stood off, the light cruiser *Sydney* and the three Destroyers preceded into the harbour to investigate – finding it completely empty.

On the night of the 11th, the force was strengthened by the arrival of the Destroyer *Encounter*. The powerful Australian force remained on station off

Rabaul as personnel attempted to locate and destroy the German W/T (Wireless/Transmitter) station without success. A threat was issued to the German authorities that Rabaul would be bombarded if they did not reveal the location of the W/T station, but again the Germans refused to reveal its location and the Australian force eventually departed without having located the W/T.

HMAS *Australia*, with other elements of the Australian Fleet, enters Simpson Harbour, Rabaul, on 12 September 1914. AWM

The force proceeded to Port Moresby, New Guinea to take on coal from Colliers, which had been dispatched to a temporary base there. Prior to reaching Port Moresby *Australia*, with other ships from the group, investigated Shortlands Harbour on the Island of Bougainville on 13 August, eventually arriving at Port Moresby on the 16th. After coaling, HMAS *Australia* and its task group departed Port Moresby on 17 August, bound for Noumea on the Island of New Caledonia; arriving there on the 21st, where they took on more coal. On the 20th, the force had been joined by the light cruiser HMAS *Melbourne* en-route to Noumea and at Noumea on the 21st joined up with the French Armoured Cruiser *Montcalm* and a RNZN (Royal New Zealand Navy) force consisting of the Destroyers *Psyche*, *Philomel* and *Pyramus* further increasing the fighting power of the group, which had already massively outgunned the German Pacific Squadron.

This powerful squadron, centered around HMAS *Australia*, departed New Caledonia and headed for Apia, Samoa, but called in at Suva, Fiji on 26 August to take on coal for the P Class Destroyers, eventually arriving off Apia around 9.00 am on 30 August. The German authorities at Apia chose not to resist the overwhelming force of the *Australia* squadron and Apia capitulated. The squadron proceeded to sweep the harbour with 'picket boats' before troops were landed to locate and destroy the W/T which had tried to transmit a message warning of the arrival of the allied force before the Germans themselves burned the station.

On 31 August, the light cruiser *Melbourne* and the French Armoured Cruiser *Montcalm* departed, bound for Suva to take on coal where the *Sealark*, a small German vessel, was located mining the entrance. HMAS *Melbourne* was then dispatched to locate and destroy the W/T on Nauru Island while the *Montcalm* weighed for Noumea.

With elements of the HMAS *Australia* squadron now split up, the force preceded from Apia to Rossel Island, New Guinea, again rendezvousing with HMAS *Sydney*, *Encounter*, the forces three Destroyers, the Submarines *AE.1* and *AE.2*, a store ship, a Collier and the transport ship *Berrima*, which was carrying Australian troops. This force then steamed for Rabaul to land the troops as an occupation force.

The Allied force's return to Rabaul was opposed by the small German force that could be mustered for its defense, with the W/T station apparently fortified, and a number of mines laid on the various tracks. However, after two days fighting in the surrounding jungle, Rabaul was surrendered, removing it as a potential stop-over base for the German Cruiser Squadron. One casualty of the Rabaul operation occurred when the Submarine *AE.1* disappeared while on a patrol to the southward outside Rabaul on the 14th. The last sighting of her was on her return from patrol at 3.30 pm that day.

Following the Rabaul operation HMAS *Australia* and HMAS *Sydney* were ordered to make for Sydney, Australia. They were to be joined at Sydney by HMAS *Melbourne*, which would be delayed as it was conducting a search for the Submarine *AE.1*. As HMAS *Australia* and *Sydney* left Rabaul the French Armoured Cruiser *Montcalm* arrived to guard the base against possible attack by the German Cruiser Squadron. After only a short time into the Voyage to Sydney, in the vicinity of Rossel Island, the *Australia* and the *Sydney* were both ordered to quickly return to Rabaul as information had been received that the German Armoured Cruisers *Gneisenau* and *Scharnhorst*, and possibly the light Cruisers from the squadron, were at Samoa. After coaling from the Colliers at Rabaul the *Australia, Encounter, Berrima* and the *Montcalm* departed for Frederick Wilhelmshaven, New Guinea, which was captured without any resistance, as the small force previously available to the Germans had been sent to Rabaul to bolster that stations defenses. The *Sydney* detached to proceed to Angaur in the Pelew Islands, with orders to destroy the W/T station located there.

The *Australia* and the other ships in the force returned to Rabaul, after a small garrison had been left at Frederick Wilhelmshaven. At Rabaul, the *Australia* again coaled from the Colliers before going on to Ponape (also known as Pohnpei) in the Caroline Islands in company with the *Montcalm*. When some 200 miles out from Rabaul the *Australia* was informed that the German Armoured Cruisers had been noted at Tahiti. This news prompted the *Australia* and

Montcalm to again return to Rabaul.

It was decided to move the allied force to Suva, which was to become the main base and the *Australia* proceeded to Suva with the *Sydney* and *Montcalm* while HMAS *Encounter* and the Destroyers were tasked with escorting Submarine *AE.2*, the transport and Colliers to Suva via Noumea. The *River Class* Torpedo Boat Destroyer HMAS *Yarra* had to be towed to Sydney by the *Berrima* after damaging a propeller on an uncharted rock or reef. The force operated from Suva for the next three weeks, patrolling the various sea routes and coming back to Suva to coal.

On 5 November 1914, while on one such patrol on the New Zealand Suva route, the *Australia* was informed about the battle of Coronel, in which the German Cruiser squadron, minus the *SMS Emden*, had defeated a British Cruiser squadron off the west coast of Chile in the South Pacific. The *Australia* was ordered to return to Suva, joining up with the fast Collier *Malina*, and then preceded to Fanning Island. Arriving in daylight, the *Australia* coaled from the Collier and departed Fanning Island that same night, bound for Magdalena Bay in southern California, USA.

The *Town Class* Light Cruiser HMS *Newcastle* signaled HMAS *Australia* on the 20th ordering her to change destination for Chamela Bay, Mexico, where she was to join up with the *Newcastle* and three Japanese Navy vessels, the *Asama*, *Idzuma* and *Hizen*. As her Collier had been ordered south to Pinyas Bay (probably Pinas Bay), the *Australia* coaled from another Collier at Chamela Bay. Bad weather delayed the coaling and *Australia* did not depart until the evening of 27 November. In company with the *Newcastle* and other ships of this inter-Allied squadron the *Australia* proceeded to the Galapagos Islands where she coaled, while the *Newcastle* was dispatched to the Coco's Islands before the ships sailed for Pinyas Bay in Columbia. One day before arriving at Pinyas Bay, the squadron was informed of the destruction of the German Cruiser Squadron by a British Squadron off the Falkland Islands. This news was effectively the catalyst for bringing *Australia's* Pacific operations to an end as her firepower would no longer be required now that the German Armoured Cruisers had been sunk.

Australia detached from the *Newcastle* and Japanese warships and departed Pinyas Bay bound for Panama where she was expected to transit the Panama Canal and enter the Atlantic Ocean side before proceeding to Jamaica. However, a landslide at the canal meant that she could not transit through and she returned to Pinyas Bay to take on coal before again departing, leaving the *Newcastle* and Japanese ships of the North Pacific Squadron at Pinyas for a second time as the *Australia* sailed south with the intention of rounding the horn. She called at Callao for stores before continuing south and altering course when somewhere south of Iquique, Northern Chile, and proceeding to St Felix Island in order to communicate with a pair of Japanese Colliers which had been left there without communications. The *Australia* then proceeded to Valparaiso,

Chile to take on coal from Lighters. On arrival at Valparaiso the *Australia* was informed that the German transport *Prinz Eitel* had departed the previous day on a northerly heading. The *Australia* took some 24 hours to coal before departing Valparaiso and heading south where she met up with HMS *Kent* and *Orama*, which were proceeding North accompanied by a pair of Colliers, on 29 December.

Australia entered the Magellan Straits early on 31 December, where she stopped to communicate with HMS *Carnarvon* off Cape Forward. She then anchored between the first and second Narrows around 8.00 pm. At 2.00 am, as daylight was breaking on 1 January 1915, Australia weighed and departed for Port Stanley in the Falkland Islands

Following a one day delay, due to a propeller blade repair, *Australia* departed Port Stanly on 5 January 1915. This proved fortunate, for the following day she sighted a small steamer which was stopped by firing a single 12-in shell at a range of 16,000 yards at 5.00 pm just as the south Atlantic dusk was closing in. The vessel was identified as the 5,000 ton German collier *Eleonore Woerman* carrying a cargo of coal and stores from St George's Bay and bound for Swakopmund in German South West Africa. Her crew was taken aboard the *Australia* before she was sunk by two 12-in common and four 4-in lyddite shells, following which *Australia* steamed for Abrolhos Rock, Brazil, arriving there at midnight on 11 January 1915, where she took on coal before departing at 5.00 pm on the 12th, bound for St Vincent in the Cape Verd Islands, going via Fernando Noronha Island where it was hoped that the German Steamer *Kron Prinz Wilhelm* was. Without sighting the *Kron Prinz Wilhelm*, *Australia* arrived at St Vincent to take on coal before sailing for Plymouth, United Kingdom, arriving at 02.00 am on 28 January 1915, bringing to an end her wartime operations before joining the Grand Fleet in British Home Waters.

On her arrival in the UK she docked at Devonport until 12 February when she sailed bound for Rosyth on the River Forth, where she was to join the 2nd Battle Cruiser Squadron. During her passage to Rosyth, *Australia* took the route around Ireland and the Shetland Islands off the North of Scotland, enduring a gale en-route, before arriving at Rosyth on 17 February 1915. At Rosyth she completed a short refit before joining the 2nd Battle Cruiser Squadron and assuming the flagship role on 22 February, still flying the flag of Vice Admiral G.E. Patey. However, Vice Admiral Patey was replaced by Rear-Admiral W.C. Pakenham as commanding officer of the 2nd Battle Cruiser Squadron on 7 March 1915, flying his flag in the *Australia*. Although commander of 2nd Battle Cruiser Squadron with his Flag in HMAS *Australia*, the de-facto Australian fleet Flagship, Rear-Admiral Pakenham was not the commander of the Australian Fleet. The 2nd Battle Cruiser Squadron comprised *Australia's* sister ships HMS *New Zealand* and HMS *Indefatigable*.

4

THE NORTH SEA AND ATLANTIC - AUGUST 1914 TO 31 DECEMBER 1914

When Great Britain declared war on Germany on 4 August 1914, the Royal Navy had nine Battlecruisers in commission (this includes HMAS *Australia*, which was owned and operated by the Royal Australian Navy, but was put under British Admiralty control for the duration of the war) and a tenth, HMS *Tiger*, close to completion. The three *Invincible Class*, HMS *Invincible, Inflexible and Indomitable* and the three *Indefatigable Class* vessels, HMS *Indefatigable*, HMS *New Zealand* and HMAS *Australia*, were each armed with a main battery of eight x 12-in guns, while the three *Lion Class*, HMS *Lion*, HMS *Princess Royal and* HMS *Queen Mary* (HMS *Queen Mary* was actually a sub-Class of the of the *Lion* design, differing in a number of details from the other two vessels) and the incomplete HMS *Tiger* (*Tiger* was a single Class vessel) were armed with a main battery of eight x 13.5-in guns. In comparison, Germany had only four Battlecruisers in commission, SMS *Von der Tann, Moltke, Goeben* and *Seydlitz*, with two others SMS *Lutzow* and *Derfflinger* still building, but close to completion. In addition, SMS *Blucher* was often counted as part of Germanys' Battle Cruiser Force, although it was little more than a modern Armoured Cruiser armed with a battery of twelve x 8.2-in guns.

The Royal Navy also held a numerical advantage in Battleships, Light Cruiser and Destroyers.

As the last days of peace counted down to war, *SMS Blucher* was employed as a gunnery training ship, while the *Goeben* was stationed in the Adriatic and Mediterranean Sea, leaving only *Von der Tann, Moltk*e and *Seydlitz* immediately available for operations with the German High Seas Fleet in the North Sea. The Royal Navy had three Battlecruisers, HMS *Inflexible, Indomitable* and *Indefatigable* operating out of Malta in the Mediterranean Sea, while HMAS *Australia* was on the other side of the World and would operate in the Pacific region during the early months of the war.

In home waters, HMS *Invincible* had just completed a refit and re-commissioned into the 2nd Battle Cruiser Squadron on 3 August 1914, literally on the eve of war (some sources suggest she completed her refit on 6 August, but official records show the date as 3 August) and the following day Great Britain declared war on Germany. *Invincible* apparently went to Queenstown as part of the Royal Navy's trade protection measures before returning to home waters in mid August. Here she was allocated as flagship of the 2nd Battle Cruiser Squadron, flying the flag of Rear Admiral H. G. H. W. Moore, then commander of the 2nd Battle Cruiser Squadron (again there are conflicting dates of 12 and 19 August 1914 for her assuming her flagship role).

The German High Seas Fleet, which was concentrated so as to threaten Britain in the North Sea, was commanded by Admiral von Ingenohl, who had taken command in February 1913, flying his flag in the Battleship *SMS Friedrich der Grosse*. He commanded a powerful force, consisting of three squadrons of Battleships as well as the Battle Cruiser Force.

Squadron I comprised of the 'Dreadnought' type Battleships *Ostfriesland, Thuringen, Helgoland, Oldenburg, Posen, Rheinland, Nassau* and *Westfalen* commanded by Vice-Admiral Von Lansa, with Rear-Admiral Gaedecke as his second in command. Squadron II comprised the 'Pre-Dreadnought' type Battleships *Preussen, Schlesien, Hessen, Lothringen, Hannover, Schleswig-Holstein, Pommern* and *Deutschland* commanded by Vice-Admiral Scheer, with Commodore Mauve as second in command. Squadron III, commanded by Rear-Admiral Funke, comprised the 'Dreadnought' type Battleships *SMS Kaiser, Kaiserin, Konig Albert* and *Prinz Regent Luitpold*.

The Cruiser force was commanded by Rear Admiral Hipper, with Rear Admiral Maass as second in command. This force, which would become the Scouting Force, comprised the Battle Cruisers *Von der Tann, Moltke* and *Seydlitz*, Light Cruisers SMS *Koln, Mainz, Stralsund, Kolberg, Rostock* and *Strassburg* and seven Destroyer Flotillas', which would come under the command of the High Seas Fleet, although a number of these were not commanded by the High Seas Fleet prior to war breaking out. There were also three Tenders, the *Hela*, which was a small obsolete Cruiser and the *Blitz* and *Pfeil*.

To counter the powerful German Fleet, the Royal Navy boasted the most powerful Battle Fleet the world had yet seen. Her two navy policy (maintaining a fleet at least as powerful as the next two most powerful fleets in the world combined) had ensured the Royal Navy an overwhelming force, which could be deployed to counter the German Fleet in the North Sea. Commanded by Admiral (from 4 August) John Jellicoe flying his flag in the *Iron Duke Class* Battleship HMS *Iron Duke*, the Grand Fleet was prepared for war in the last days of July 1914.

HMS *Lion* was Beatty's Flagship when it was part of the 1st Battle Cruiser Squadron and continued its Flagship role when the Battle Cruiser Fleet was formed in early 1915.

In early 1914, Jellicoe was at the Admiralty serving in the capacity of Second Sea Lord - having held this post since December 1912 - when he was offered and subsequently accepted the position of Commander of the Home Fleets, which was due to be changed under the normal rotation in December 1914, when the then Commander of the Home Fleets, Admiral Sir George Callaghan was scheduled to stand down. Normally the position would be held for two years at a time, but Admiral Callaghan's term was extended by the Admiralty in 1913, having first been appointed to the post in 1910.

As international tensions increased in mid-July 1914, Jellicoe was informed by the First Lord, Mr. Winston Churchill that if hostilities broke out involving Britain then it would be necessary for the Commander of the Home Fleets to be assisted by a "Second in Command," appointing Jellicoe to this position. Consultations with Admiral Callaghan followed regarding many issues, not least of which was what ship Jellicoe would fly his flag from, with the *King George the V* Class Battleship HMS *Centurion* being decided upon. On 29 and 30 July, meetings were held at the Admiralty regarding the various dispositions of the Fleets among other issues discussed.

In preparation for commencing his duties as Second in Command of the Home Fleets, Jellicoe officially stood down as Second Sea Lord on 30 July, with Vice-Admiral Sir Frederick Hamilton, K.C.B. taking over this post. The following day, 31 July, Jellicoe, while at the Admiralty had a conversation with the First Sea Lord, the Marquis of Milford Haven and the First Lord, Mr. Churchill. It was now that it was suggested to him that in "in certain circumstances," obviously meaning the outbreak of war, that Jellicoe could succeed Admiral Callaghan as Commander-in-Chief Home Fleets. The surprise at this information was followed by a protest from Jellicoe at such a move being considered at a time when war could break out any day. Jellicoe's concerns were that replacing the Commander-in-Chief virtually on the eve of probable war was not a sound move as the current Commander was "in-touch with the fleet," and had considerable experience of commanding such a large fleet. In a telegram, Jellicoe put forward the suggestion that Admiral Callaghan remain and Jellicoe act as his assistant aboard the Flagship.

In the North Sea Theatre the German High Sea's Fleet operated a smaller, but powerful force of Battle Cruisers. The SMS *Von der Tann* was the first true Battle Cruiser built in Germany

With no decision yet taken, Jellicoe departed by train for Wick in Northern Scotland, where he was to be met by the *Boadicea Class* Scout Cruiser HMS *Boadicea*, which would take him to the fleet at Scapa Flow. Due to a prevailing fog, HMS *Boadicea* could not depart from Wick until 2 August, with Jellicoe arriving at Scapa Flow that afternoon.

Around 4.00 am on the morning of 4 August, Jellicoe received Admiralty orders to open an envelope containing secret orders he had carried with him from London. On opening the orders, Jellicoe was confirmed as the new Commander-in-Chief of the Grand Fleet, which superseded the Home Fleets then in existence. He then proceeded aboard the Flagship, HMS *Iron Duke* and was informed that Admiral Callaghan had received Admiralty orders to relinquish command and hand over to Jellicoe. In later writings Jellicoe would describe the anguish, which he felt at the way in which he was taking over command from a man whom he deeply respected and considered a friend. Initially it was planned for command to change to Jellicoe on the 5th of August, however, an alert to make ready for sea on the morning of the 4th compelled them to decide it was better if command was passed over quicker, and subsequently Admiral Callaghan lowered his Flag on HMS *Iron Duke* at 08.20 am on 4 August before disembarking. The Fleet was now officially under the command of Admiral Jellicoe.

On 4 August 1914 the strength of the Grand Fleet Battleship, Battle Cruiser, Cruisers, Light Cruisers and Destroyer fleets was as follows

Dreadnought and Super Dreadnought Battleships	20
Pre-Dreadnought Battleships	8
Battle Cruisers	4
Armoured Cruisers	8
Light Cruisers (modern)	13
Flotilla Leaders	1
Destroyers (new modern)	77
Destroyers (old)	8

Warships stationed in home waters, but not part of the Grand Fleet

Pre-Dreadnought Battleships	30
Armoured Cruisers	9
Destroyers (new modern)	14
Destroyers (old)	85
Torpedo boats (oil burning)	36
Submarines	61

In addition to these forces there were hundreds of smaller craft, ranging from Sloops, Trawlers down to small harbor patrol boats for a diversity of duties such as harbor patrol and minesweeping. There were also large numbers of warships operating in various stations throughout the world including a number of Pre-Dreadnought Type Battleships, Armoured Cruisers, Light Cruisers, Destroyers and the three Battlecruisers, which were operating in the Mediterranean.

On the outbreak of war in August 1914, the Grand Fleet was a much superior force to that which it opposed. The strength and organisation was as follows:

Flagship of the Fleet - HMS *Iron Duke* (*Iron Duke Class* Super Dreadnought) flying the Flag of Admiral John Jellicoe

1st Battle Squadron - commanded by Vice-Admiral Sir Lewis Bayly, K.C.B, with Rear-Admiral H. Evan Thomas as 2nd in command.

HMS *Marlborough* (Flagship), HMS *St Vincent* (Rear Flagship), HMS *Colossus*, HMS *Hercules*, HMS *Neptune*, HMS *Vanguard*, HMS *Collingwood*, HMS *Superb*, HMS *Bellona* (Light Cruiser attached to Squadron), HMS *Cyclops* (repair vessel).

2nd Battle Squadron - commanded by Vice-Admiral Sir George Warraender, Bart., K.C.B., with Rear-Admiral Sir Robert Arbuthnot, Bart as 2nd in command.

HMS *King George V* (Flagship), HMS *Orion* (Rear-Flagship), HMS *Ajax*, HMS *Audacious*, HMS *Centurion*, HMS *Conqueror*, HMS *Monarch*, HMS *Thunderer*, the Light Cruiser HMS *Boadicea* (Light Cruiser attached to Squadron) and HMS *Assistance* (Repair vessel).

4th Battle Squadron - commanded by Vice-Admiral Sir Douglas Gamble, K.C.V.O.

HMS *Dreadnought* (Flagship), HMS *Temaraire*, HMS *Bellerophon* and Light Cruiser HMS *Blonde* (Light Cruiser attached to squadron).

3rd Battle Squadron (Pre-Dreadnoughts) - commanded by Vice-Admiral E.E. Bradford, C.V.O., with Rear-Admiral M.E. Browning as 2nd in command.

HMS *King Edward VII* (Flagship), HMS *Hibernia* (Rear-Flagship), HMS *Commonwealth*, HMS *Zealandia*, HMS *Dominion*, HMS *Africa*, HMS *Britannia*, HMS *Hindustan* and HMS *Blanche* (Light Cruiser attached to squadron).

1st Battle Cruiser Squadron - commanded by Vice-Admiral (acting) Sir David Beatty.

HMS *Lion* (Flagship), HMS *Princess Royal*, HMS *Queen Mary* and HMS *New Zealand*.

2nd Cruiser Squadron - commanded by Rear-Admiral the Hon. S. Gouth-Calthorpe

HMS *Shannon* (*Minotaur* Class Armoured Cruiser; Flagship), HMS *Achilles* (*Warrior* Class Armoured Cruiser), HMS *Cochrane* (*Warrior* Class Armoured Cruiser) and HMS *Natal* (*Warrior* Class Armoured Cruiser)

3rd Cruiser Squadron - commanded by Rear-Admiral W.C. Pekenham, C.B.

HMS *Antrim* (Flagship), HMS *Argyll*, HMS *Devonshire*, HMS *Roxburgh* (all *Devonshire* Class Armoured Cruisers).

1st Light Cruiser Squadron - commanded by Commodore W.E. Goodenough

HMS *Southampton* (Flagship), HMS *Birmingham*, HMS *Lowestoft*, HMS *Nottingham* (Town Class)

Second Destroyer Flotilla - commanded by Captain J.R.P. Hawkesly

HMS *Active* (Flotilla command ship), HMS *Acorn*, HMS *Alarm*, HMS *Brisk*, HMS *Cameleon*, HMS *Comet*, HMS *Fury*, HMS *Goldfinch*, HMS *Hope*, HMS *Larne*, HMS *Lyra*, HMS *Martin*, HMS *Minstrel*, HMS *Nemesis*, HMS *Nereide*, HMS *Nymphe*, HMS *Redpole*, HMS *Rifleman*, HMS *Ruby*, HMS *Sheldrake* and *HMS Staunch*.

Fourth Destroyer Flotilla

HMS *Acasta*, HMS *Achates*, HMS *Ambuscade*, HMS *Ardent*, HMS *Christoppher*, HMS *Cockatrice*, HMS *Contest*, HMS *Fortune*, HMS *Garland*, HMS *Hardy*, HMS *Lynx*, HMS *Midge*, HMS *Owl*, HMS *Paragon*, HMS *Porpoise*, HMS *Shark*, HMS *Sparrowhawk*, HMS *Spitfire*, HMS *Unity* and HMS *Victor*.

Minesweeping Gunboats

HMS *Skipjack* (Senior Officers ship; initially absent from fleet), HMS *Circe*, HMS *Grossamer*, HMS *Leda*, HMS *Speedwell*, HMS *Jason* and HMS *Seagull*.

The Shetland Patrol Force consisted of HMS *Forward* (*Scout Class* Light Cruiser) and four *River Class* Destroyers.

The Commander-in-Chief also had operational command over several other forces including the Harwich Force and the Second and Third Fleets based in Southern British Ports.

The Harwich Force consisted of the following:

1st Destroyer Flotilla under the Command of Captain W. Blunt in the Flotilla Leader *HMS Fearless* (*Active Class* Scout Cruiser), Flotilla Leader for the force of 20 Destroyers.

3rd Destroyer Flotilla commanded by Captain C.H. Fox in HMS *Amphion* (*Active Class* Scout Cruiser), Flotilla Leader for the force of 15 Destroyers.

The Second Fleet was commanded by Vice-Admiral Sir Cecil Burney, K.C.B., K.C.M.G.

HMS *Lord Nelson* (*Lord Nelson Class Battleship*; the last Class of Pre-Dreadnought's built for the Royal Navy) was the Second Fleet's Flagship for Rear-Admirals Stuart Nicholson and Bernard Curry commanding the fleets two Battle Squadrons.

5th Battle Squadron - HMS *Prince of Wales* (Flagship), HMS *Agamemnon*, HMS *Bulwark*, HMS *Formidable*, HMS *Implacable* HMS *Irresistible*, HMS *London*, HMS *Queen* and HMS *Venerable*.

6th Battle Squadron - HMS *Russell* (Flagship), HMS *Cornwallis*, HMS *Albemarle*, HMS *Duncan*, HMS *Exmouth* and HMS *Vengeance*.

5th Cruiser Squadron - commanded by Rear-Admiral A.P. Stoddart

HMS *Carnarvon* –Flagship – (*Devonshire Class* Armoured Cruiser), HMS *Falmouth* and HMS *Liverpool* (both *Town Class* Light Cruisers).

6th Cruiser Squadron - commanded by Rear-Admiral W.L. Grant

HMS *Drake*, HMS *Good Hope*, HMS *King Alfred*, HMS *Leviathan* (all *Drake Class* Armoured Cruisers)

In general, the Royal Navy had four main tasks in the event of war with a major power.

1: Ensuring the seaways were passable for British Merchant shipping, which would be required to bring in huge quantities of materials, particularly food for the nation, which was not self sufficient, particularly in regards to the food required to feed its population.
2: Blockade of enemy ports in order to force economic pressure on his economy and prevent essential supplies getting through.
3: To provide escort for the transport of the Army overseas and provide ongoing protection to its sea lines of communications and supply and reinforcement routes to and from the United Kingdom.
4: To stand guard to engage and defeat any hostile nations attempt to invade the United Kingdom and any of its Dominions and Territories overseas.

To ensure the seaways were safe for British Shipping and reduce, if not entirely remove the threat of invasion of the parent country, the obvious first task was to seek to engage and destroy the enemy's Battle Fleet by employing the Royal Navy's advantage of overwhelming force. However, history should have taught that bringing a reluctant enemy to a decisive fleet action would be no easy task. During the Napoleonic Wars of the early 19th Century the Royal Navy for much of the time took on the role of sentry as the weaker enemy forces opted to stay in harbour, when the alternative was to put to Sea and be destroyed or captured. This involved keeping naval Squadrons at sea off the enemy's ports, effectively bottling them up in port.

For the Royal Navy in 1914 the problems would be similar. Faced with an enemy unwilling to expose its smaller, weaker Battle Fleet to a fleet action, which would be overwhelmingly tipped against them, the problem was how to stand guard over this very dangerous threat to the nation's survival. For the Germans, it was entirely the right policy to keep its Battle Fleet intact as a dagger pointed at Britain's throat, while looking for ways to try and reduce the British superiority in numbers through a war of attrition. This policy would be stacked in Germanys' favour as the Royal Navy would have to maintain a high tempo of operations at sea, exposing itself to the new weapons of the Mine and Torpedo, while the main body of the German Fleet remained safe in its fortified fortress harbours. That said any lengthy periods of inactivity for the German Fleet, as with any fleet, would have detrimental effects on efficiency and moral of the crews.

It was the new weapons; the Mine and Torpedo, combined with aircraft, which initially meant the Royal Navy could not simply stand off the enemy's fortified harbours and keep him bottled up. This would allow the Germans a measure of freedom to break out into the North Sea, either unknown to the British, or at least with the advantage of being well out to sea before they were discovered. This would serve the Germans well in some minor bombardments of the British East Coast, which would bring extreme embarrassment upon the Grand Fleet, which had many difficulties in its attempts to intercept the Germans before they retired to their fortified sanctuaries.

As recounted later, the force with the best chance of intercepting these German ventures to the British East Coast was the Royal Navy's Battle Cruiser Squadrons supported by Light Cruisers, due to their high speed in comparison to the Battle Fleet, and to the fact that they were based at Rosyth on the River Forth Estuary, considerably further south than the main Grand Fleet anchorages at Scapa Flow and Cromarty. However, in moving to intercept the German bombardment forces the British Battlecruisers would risk being drawn onto the German main Battle Fleet and severely damaged or destroyed, which of course was the main tactic employed by the German High Seas Fleet in the first half of the war.

The Grand Fleet, therefore, would have to sail in support of the Battle Cruiser Force, although its northern anchorage and slower speed would mean that it would be unlikely to be in position to engage the German Fleet unless some advance warning of an operation were available. This would mean the Battle Cruiser Force would have to use its best judgment during an engagement with German Forces attempting to bring the British onto the guns of the High Sea's Fleet.

The Grand Fleet was deficient in the number of Destroyers that were required to provide a constant screen for both the Battle Fleet and the Battle Cruiser Squadron if kept continually at sea. The number required for the Battle Fleet alone was considered to be 40 Destroyers and this was the number that was available for both the Battle Fleet and Battle Cruiser Squadron. The relatively short endurance of the Destroyers allowed then to remain at sea for around three full days, whereas the Capital ships could remain at sea for up to three times longer.

As the ominous blackness of war clouds gathered over Europe, the main British Fleet had moved north to Scapa Flow in the last days of July 1914. This was not simply a knee jerk reaction, but a sound policy as the Admiralty had decided a few years before the outbreak of war that Scapa Flow would become the main British Fleet base in the event of a war with Germany. The distance from Scapa Flow to the main German bases in Jade Estuary of around 450 miles certainly put it within the range of German Destroyers as well as Submarines. While the navigational hazards of the channels into the anchorage were always going to be the main defences against Submarine attack, the vital Gun defences decided upon to counter an attack by surface craft had never been implemented due to financial constraints.

As the fleet moved to Scapa in late July, the best that could be done to increase defence against surface attack was to land a number of 12 pounder guns from British ships and position them at the entrance, albeit without searchlights, effectively rendering them all but useless at night. In addition, some Light Cruisers and Destroyers were placed at various entrances to supplement these meager defences. Once the fleet was in place additional measures were taken including patrols in the area eastward of the Pentland Firth, which was of limited defensive value.

The bases further to the south were better protected, although by no means fortified. The base at Cromarty was served by a single, relatively narrow entrance and was defended by a number of guns making it hazardous for an enemy surface force to approach. On the negative side, it completely lacked a boom defence against the entry of a Destroyer force willing to take casualties from the gun defences. Its Submarine defences were to all extent and purposes non-existent, with no real obstruction even in the narrow entry channel. During the first few months of the war the defences of the main anchorages were increased against both surface and sub-surface attack.

From the outset of war, a major problem for the German Navy was the security of the Heligoland Bight region. Vice Admiral Hipper, commander of the German Scouting Forces, which included the Battle Cruisers was tasked with providing a defensive system in the Heligoland Bight, which was planned to give the German's enough notice of a British advance into the Bight in force to allow various countermeasures to be taken. The problems for the Germans were many: The farther out from her bases the defensive arc began, the less well it could be monitored or defended and the more ships would be required to patrol it. There were a number of defensive arcs. During daylight hours an outer defense line was located about 35 nautical miles out from the lightship *Elbe I*. This line of just over 1,800 meters was patrolled by a number of Torpedo Boat Destroyers, while about six nautical miles behind this was another line, which was patrolled by Submarines, with a third line about six miles behind this patrolled by Mine-Sweepers of the Mine Sweeping Divisions. Backing up these defensive lines was between two and four Light Cruisers, which were positioned on the flanks of the defensive arc, east and south of Heligoland. During the hours of darkness the system was changed and only the innermost line was patrolled, with the Submarines and Destroyers of the two outermost lines returning to base.

The various patrol lines were designed as a purely defensive measure against a Royal Navy advance into the Heligoland Bight in force, but it took up valuable resources in light forces and Submarines, which could not conduct their main role of offensive operations against enemy forces at sea. Nor was it in any real way a system to give adequate intelligence information in regards British movements in the North Sea as its out perimeter extended out only around 35 miles. For long-range reconnaissance, the Germans relied mainly on aircraft and Zeppelins. However, in the early days of the war there were only around five aircraft available at the aerodrome at Heligoland and only a single Zeppelin, L3 was available.

Even as a defensive system, it was recognised that it was less than ideal, as at 35 nautical miles out Destroyers on the outermost patrol line, even in conditions of good visibility, may spot British large units at a distance of between ten and fifteen miles. This would allow these heavy units to come within the range of the Heligoland Fortress in about one hour and 30 minutes to one hour and 45 minutes after detection, assuming the British ships were steaming at full speed. In such case, the Germans would probably only have been able to get their ships which were lying in the outer Jade out into the open sea, as a longer period of time would be required for vessels lying in the River Elbe at Cuxhaven or the base at Wilhelmshaven Roads in the Jade to make the open sea. Therefore, if the British Grand Fleet advanced on the Heligoland Bight the Germans would be in a position whereby they would only be capable of meeting it with a much reduced force. Airborne reconnaissance was, therefore, completely essential to the German defensive measures against a British advance into the Heligoland Bight.

With war declared on Germany, the Royal Navy continued and reinforced its patrols and defensive measures in the North Sea and along the British coast. Harbours and anchorages were also having defences increased, particularly at vulnerable strategic locations such as Rosyth in the Firth of Forth, which would become home to the Battlecruiser forces. The Germans to, were busy increasing their defenses, which also included planned laying of minefields near the British coast as part of Germany's policy of trying to inflict losses of British warships at little or no cost to themselves in an attempt to reduce the Royal navy's superiority in ship numbers.

In the lead-up to the outbreak of war the Admiralty received a number of reports about German shipping. One such report indicated that three German merchant ships had been observed passing the 'Great Belt' sometime on the evening of 1 August. The commander-in-chief (presumably the previous Commander in Chief) had ordered the 1st Battle Cruiser Squadron and the 3rd Cruiser Squadron consisting of the Armoured Cruisers HMS *Cochrane* and *Achilles* of the *Duke of Edinburgh* Class (*Achilles* was from the *Warrior* Sub-Class of the *Duke of Edinburgh* Class) to proceed to sea during the evening of 3 August. These units were to patrol south of the Fair Island Channel throughout that night.

Under the new Commander in Chief, the Grand Fleet put to sea from Scapa Flow at 08.30 am on the morning of 4 August 1914. Jellicoe flew his flag in HMS *Iron Duke* and was accompanied by the Battleships of the 1st, 2nd, 3rd and

4th Battle Squadrons, the 1st Battle Cruiser Squadron and the Light Cruisers HMS *Birmingham, Southampton, Boadicea* and *Blonde* along with the Destroyers of the 4th Flotilla. Sailing from Rosyth, on the Forth Estuary, were the Armoured Cruisers HMS *Shannon, Natal* and *Roxburgh*, the Light Cruisers HMS *Nottingham, Falmouth* and *Liverpool* and the 2nd Destroyer Flotilla. Two Light Cruisers (Scout Cruisers), HMS *Bellona* and *Blanche* remained in port as they were still coaling. This force was instructed to rendezvous with the Grand Fleet main body at Latitude 58.40 N., Longitude 1.30 E.

The German Auxiliary Cruiser *Kronprinz Friedrich Wilhelm* put to sea on 4 August, followed by the Auxiliary Minelayer *Konigin Luise*, commanded by Commander Biermann, which departed the Ems at 9.30 pm bound for the Thames Estuary with the wireless signal "Make for sea in Thames direction at top speed. Lay mines near as possible English coasts, not near neutral coasts, and not farther north than Lat 53°. After laying a number of mines *Konigin Luise* was detected and engaged by British Light Cruisers and Destroyers around 11.00 am on 5 August, and was quickly sunk by a torpedo. However, one of the mines laid by the *Konigin Luise* was struck by the Royal Navy Cruiser HMS *Amphion*, which subsequently sank.

These sailings were the first operations of the German High Seas Fleet War orders to try and inflict casualties on the Royal Navy through a serious of operations that would not risk the fleet to open conflict with a vastly superior force. The Germans had succeeded in inflicting the loss of a Cruiser on the Royal Navy, but had lost an Auxiliary Mine laying Cruiser in the process. Judged a successful operation by the Germans, it was equally a successful interception by the Royal Navy of the first German surface operation towards Britain's coasts of the war, albeit at the cost of one Cruiser sunk.

During the first week of the war both sides used Submarines for reconnaissance purposes, with each side attempting to glean information about the others defensive patrols and minefields. The Germans also launched an offensive operation using Submarines against potential British Battle Fleet movements into the North Sea, but this yielded nothing and the Submarines returned to base by 11 August, although two were reported lost. Over the next few weeks both sides continued their patrols using light surface forces and Submarines, with attacks on their respective fishing fleets being conducted as well as minefields being laid. On at least one occasion in the first weeks British Destroyers met a German Light Cruiser, but turned away after exchanging fire and were soon out of range of the German warship.

Towards the last week of August 1914, the Royal Navy had five operational Battlecruisers in home waters, HMS *Lion, Princess Royal, Queen Mary, New Zealand* and *Invincible,* with the new *Tiger* Class Battlecruiser HMS *Tiger* close to joining the fleet. In addition, HMS *Inflexible* had been ordered back to home waters from the Mediterranean on 18/19 August to bolster the British position in the

North Sea. There had been no challenge to British dominance of the North Sea by the heavy units of the German High Seas Fleet and the British remained in control of the high seas the world over, with little interference by the German warships at large outside European Waters. This enabled Britain to continue to transport goods and personnel from all parts of the world and at home. Absolute dominance in the English Channel allowed the transport of the BEF (British Expeditionary Force) to France without any serious interference and no transport vessels were lost.

It remained, however, fact that it was in the North Sea that any major clash between the opposing fleets would occur. Both sides continued their defensive patrols, while looking at ways to inflict serious losses on each other at light or no cost to themselves.

The Battle of Heligoland Bight

The action, which became known as the 'Battle of Heligoland Bight' originated with a Royal Navy plan to spring an ambush on German Light Forces patrols that were regularly conducted in the Heligoland Bight. Three hours after war was declared on Germany on 4 August 1914, the Royal Navy Submarines *E.6* and *E.8* left port to conduct a reconnaissance in the area of the Heligoland Bight near the German North Sea coast. During this patrol information was gathered as to the frequency and areas of German patrols in this area.

The Submarines had observed the German patrols in the area, which appeared to be conducted twice a day by Torpedo Boat Destroyers supported by a handful of Light Cruisers; the latter tasked with protecting the Torpedo Boats from British Destroyer or Light Cruiser attacks.

The plan to spring the ambush was put forward by the Commodore (S), Roger Keyes, who was in command of British Submarines in the North Sea. This plan called for the use of two forces of Submarines and the Harwich Force, consisting of Light Cruisers and Destroyer Flotilla's under the command of Commodore (T) Reginald Tyrwhitt. The Harwich Force would attempt to position itself between the German Torpedo Boats and the German Coast and try to force them farther out to sea where they could be engaged and sunk by the Harwich Force as well as other heavier units which would be in support. One group of Submarines would be used as bait for the Torpedo Boats, while the other would be used to attack any German Reinforcements sent out to support the Torpedo Boats. One draft of the original plan also called for the Grand Fleet to be out in the North Sea acting as distant support in case any German Battle Squadrons came out.

Unable to get the Admiralty to consider the plan, the next move was to go straight to the First Lord of the Admiralty, Winston Churchill, who warmed to the plan in principal. Churchill arranged a conference for 24 August to be attended by Tyrwhitt, the First Sea Lord, Prince Louis of Battenburg, the 2nd Sea Lord, Vice Admiral Sir Fredrick Hamilton, and Chief of the Admiralty, Vice Admiral Sturdee. The latter decided that the Grand Fleet would not be required to support such an operation. Instead, HMS *Invincible* and HMS *New Zealand* and supporting Destroyers under the somewhat spurious designation Cruiser Force K, and a Cruiser Force consisting of five Armoured Cruisers would support the operation.

The Submarines *E.4, E.5* and *E.9* would form an inner cordon running north and South of the Heligoland coastline, with the aim of being in position to attack German ships coming out of Heligoland to reinforce the German Torpedo Boats or to engage any German warships that were heading back to base. This cordon was augmented by the Submarines *E.6, E.7* and *E.8*, which formed a line around 35-40 miles further to the north westward. These were the bait designed to entice the German Torpedo Boat Destroyers to continue on a course taking them further from their base. The Submarines *D.2* and *D.8* were positioned to counter potential German reinforcements, which could come out of Ems.

With the operation scheduled for 28 August, the Submarine force from the Eighth Submarine Flotilla consisting of *D.2, D.8, E.4, E.5, E.6, E.7, E.8* and *E.9,* accompanied by the Destroyers HMS *Lurcher* and *Firedrake*, sailed at Midnight on 26 August, followed by the Harwich Force of Light Cruisers and Destroyers, which sailed on the 27th. HMS *Lurcher* and *Firedrake* conducted scouting operations for the Submarines until nightfall on the 27th, when the Submarines detached and went to their respective planned operational areas.

One of the planned operations major flaws was the failure to inform the commander of the Grand Fleet, Admiral Jellico until 26 August. Although the planning of the operation had discounted the need for the Grand Fleet to sail in support, Admiral Jellico requested that he take the fleet out in support of the operation, citing concerns about such an operation being conducted so very close to the German Coast without support from heavy units. The Chief of the Admiralty declined Jellico's request, but consented that he could dispatch more Battlecruisers to support the operation. Therefore, Jellico ordered Beatty to take the 1st Battle Cruiser Squadron out in support. This powerful squadron consisted of HMS *Lion* (Flagship), *Princess Royal* and *Queen Mary* supported by the 1st Light Cruiser Squadron under the command of Admiral Goodenough. These two Squadrons provided a massive increase in the firepower available to the covering force, although lack of communication between the different forces meant that some elements of the British force were unaware of the 1st Battle Cruiser Squadron and 1st Light Cruiser Squadrons allocation to the operation. As a result of this there was some initial confusion when the 1st Light Cruiser Squadron met the Harwich Force at dawn on the 28th, although the identity of the two forces was soon established, bringing the Harwich Force up to date with the new participants in the operation. This left only the British

Submarines unaware of the 1st Battle Cruiser Squadron and 1st Light Cruiser Squadron participation.

The German Forces were based on two patrol areas, the first some 25 miles westward of Heligoland. This was patrolled by nine Torpedo Boat Destroyers from the 1st Torpedo Boat Flotilla, while the second patrol area lying around 12 miles from Heligoland was patrolled by III Minesweeper Division. Relative close support to the two patrols was provided by a number of Light Cruisers consisting of SMS *Ariadne, Frauenlob, Hela* and *Stettin*. Another Light Cruiser, SMS *Mainz* was in an area off Ems to the south of Heligoland, while a further seven or so Light Cruisers were in port, spread between Brunsbüttel and Wilhelmshaven. Although the Germans had Battlecruisers and Battleships in ports close to the operational area, these could not simply weigh and sail at a moment's notice, not least because of the low tides in the relatively shallow waters in the Heligoland Bight and surrounding areas and therefore, they would not be capable of supporting the light forces at sea.

The British Cruiser Force, commanded by Rear-Admiral H. H. Campbell, CVO, consisting of the Light Cruisers HMS *Euryalus* and *Amethyst*, the 1st and 3rd Destroyer Flotillas and the Submarine force were under the overall command of Rear-Admiral Christian. These forces took up their assigned positions during the course of the night of 27 August, and continued on towards the Heligoland Bight during the night of 27/28 August. Commodore Roger J B Keyes, commanding the Submarine force, had sailed in the Destroyer HMS *Lurcher* on the 27th to cover the passage of the Submarines to their positions off the German coast.

Within Admiral Campbell's Cruiser Force the Rear-Admiral utilised HMS *Euryalus* as his flagship. This force was tasked with the interception German warships that may have been forced westward into the North Sea.

A sweep to search for Submarines in the area that the Battlecruisers were passing through had been conducted at daybreak on the 28th by the Destroyers HMS *Lurcher* and *Firedrake* after they had detached from the Submarines force that they had been covering. Following this sweep *Lurcher* and *Firedrake* continued in the direction of Heligoland, following "in the wake" of three of the British Submarines, *E.6, E.7* and *E.8*.

These three Submarines were in effect the bait for the trap the British hoped to spring on the German patrols. They were tasked with revealing their presence to the enemy, who it was hoped would then pursue them westward. Although visibility had been reasonably good out to sea, closer to Heligoland this reduced to around 5,000 to 6,000 yards causing some worry among the Submarine crews, as this would reduce the time they would have to respond to the presence of any German warship that suddenly appeared at such close range. The problems of low visibility were added to by the calm sea.

The Light Cruiser HMS *Arethusa* (Commodore Tyrwhitt's flagship), in company with the First and Third Destroyer Flotilla's, minus the Destroyers HMS *Hornet, Hydra, Loyal* and *Tigress* had sailed at 5.00 am on 27 August. This force, which was joined by the Light Cruiser HMS *Fearless* at sea during the afternoon of the 27th, made contact with the enemy when a German Destroyer was sighted at 06.53 am on the 28th. The 4th Division of the Third Destroyer Flotilla gave chase to the German ship which quite understandably headed away from the British force. At 07.20 am HMS *Arethusa* and the Third Destroyer Flotilla engaged a number of German vessels, observed as Destroyers and Torpedo Boat's, which had turned on a course to Heligoland, with the British force trying to maneuver to cut them off. At 07.57 am *Arethusa's* force sighted a pair of Light Cruisers; one a two funnel and the other a four funnel vessel, first observed off *Arethusa's* port bow, with the closest German vessels being engaged by the British ships. The two German Cruisers and a number of the Destroyers now engaged *Arethusa*, which came under quite heavy fire lasting until 08.15 am, at which point one of the German Cruisers; the four funnel one, switched her fire to HMS *Fearless*. *Arethusa* was still engaged with the two-funnel Cruiser at relatively close range on "converging courses" with a shell from one of *Arethusa's* 6-in guns hitting the German Cruiser on the fore-bridge causing much damage and forcing the German ship to turn and head on a course for Heligoland, which could actually be seen on *Arethusa's* starboard bow. At this point the British ships were ordered by *Arethusa* to turn on a westward course with speed being reduced to 20 knots a short time later.

During the course of this engagement with the German Cruisers and Destroyers, HMS *Arethusa* was hit a number of times and was barely fit for action, with only a single 6-in gun remaining in operation. The ships remaining 6-in guns and torpedo tubes had all been put out of action temporarily. A German shell burst caused a fire opposite *Arethusa's* No.2 6-in gun on the port side causing some of *Arethusa's* ammunition to explode resulting in a huge fire, which lasted only a short time, but left the deck burning before fire control parties extinguished it.

The engagement with the German ships over, the Destroyer Flotilla's were re-formed into Divisions and continued on course at a speed of 20 knots. However, it was not long before it was obvious that *Arethusa* would be incapable of keeping up as her speed had been reduced as a result of damage received. HMS *Fearless* reported to *Arethusa* that the First Destroyer Flotilla's 3rd and 5th Divisions had engaged and sunk the "German Commodore's Destroyers." One of the British Destroyers, HMS Defender had to abandon two of her boat crews, which were left while they were rescuing survivors from one of the German Destroyers, which had been sunk when suddenly a German Light Cruiser appeared and opened fire on the British Destroyers.

The events leading to the sinking of the German destroyer commenced when the first German Light Cruiser appeared out of the mist and the British

Destroyers, led by the Flotilla Leader, switched their attention from the German Torpedo Boat Destroyers to the Light Cruiser, but four of the British Destroyers spotted a German Torpedo Boat Destroyer, the *V187* attempting to get back to Heligoland and began to chase her, opening fire and soon hitting her, which resulted a reduction of speed of the German vessel, could now do nothing to escape her assailants. The Torpedo Boat Destroyer was battered by a storm of fire from the British Destroyers, and despite a valiant effort to resist, was unable to inflict a single hit on any of the British warships, although one sailor aboard a Destroyer was apparently wounded by a rifle bullet.

Observers on-board the British Destroyers noted that the German ship was being torn to pieces by gunfire and was quickly enveloped in a thick cloud of dark smoke through which flames could be seen flickering about the vessels hull and decks. Before long the ship's hull, blackened by fire, was seen to be almost under water, at which point the British Destroyers were ordered to cease fire as some of the German crew jumped overboard and were swimming towards the British ships. The British launched lifeboats and began to rescue the German survivors, many of which were wounded, a number seriously. It was at this point that another German Light Cruiser suddenly appeared out of the mist, opening fire on the British Destroyers, which now frantically tried to get their own men back aboard, but were forced to leave one boat load behind as they turned away from the German Light Cruiser and managed to escape.

The Submarine *E.4* commanded by Lieutenant-Commander Ernest W. Leir, while submerged, observed the sinking of the German Torpedo Boat Destroyer *V187* by periscope. *E.4* observed the German Cruiser firing on the British Destroyers rescuing German survivors from *V187*, which then retired leaving boats and their crews in the water. Although *E.4* was unable to engage the German Cruiser, she surfaced and took on board the one officer and nine men from the Destroyer HMS *Defenders* boats, which had been abandoned. These boats also carried 28 German survivors from *V187*, 18 of who were badly injured. The submarines limited capacity meant they could not all be embarked, therefore, one of the two German Officers and six of the unwounded men were left along with the wounded Germans, while one German Officer and two of the unwounded Germans were taken aboard *E.4* as prisoners. The Germans, who were left in the boats, were provided with provisions and a compass to enable the boats to be navigated back to the German Coast.

On hearing the news that Commodore (S) in the Destroyer HMS *Lurcher* in company with HMS *Firedrake* was being pursued by German Light Cruisers, Tyrwhitt went to his assistance with HMS *Fearless* and the First Destroyer Flotilla at 10.00 am. By 10.37 am, no more information had been obtained and no contact made, therefore, as the ships were in vicinity of Heligoland, Tyrwhitt instructed the force to turn onto a westward course away from Heligoland. By this time HMS *Arethusa* had all of her guns back in commission, with the exception of two of her 4-in guns.

The British Destroyer Flotillas and Flotilla Leaders now joined up again, it was decided to make for home as there were not thought to be any German vessels still around. Suddenly another German Light Cruiser appeared, and was quickly pursued by the Flotilla Leaders HMS *Arethusa* and *Fearless*, accompanied by several Destroyer Divisions. The Remaining British Destroyers were about to head for home, with the lead ship of one of the Divisions damaged and with reduced speed. Suddenly another German Light Cruiser loomed out of the mist, and the eight British Destroyers immediately moved to attack the German warship.

A four funnel German Cruiser was sighted at 10.55 am, opening fire on *Arethusa* at 11.00 am. With *Arethusa's* situation "critical", Tyrwhitt instructed HMS *Fearless* to engage the German Cruiser with gunfire and for the First Destroyer Flotilla to attack her with torpedoes. Faced with these determined multi-pronged attacks, the German Light Cruiser turned away and steamed into a haze bank allowing her to escape the British ships. Within about ten minutes, the German Cruiser suddenly re-appeared on *Arethusa's* starboard quarter and was immediately engaged by *Arethusa* and *Fearless*, the former firing on her with both 6-in guns. A Division of Destroyers launched a torpedo attack on the German Cruiser, although none hit. Around this time Tyrwhitt reported the situation to Admiral Beatty commanding the Battlecruiser squadron in HMS *Lion*.

The German Cruiser continued to engage *Arethusa*, with many salvoes failing between 10 and 30 yards short, although she received no hits. During this phase *Arethusa* also claimed to have spotted two torpedoes launched against her, although these were well short. The combined fire of *Arethusa* and *Fearless* inflicted much damage on the German Cruiser, forcing her to turn and head for off in the direction of Heligoland. Around four minutes later a three funneled German Light Cruiser was sighted, this being the SMS *Mainz*, which was engaged by *Arethusa* and *Fearless* and a number of the British Destroyers. After 25 minutes under the withering hail of British gunfire the *Mainz* was observed to be on fire and sinking by the head and her engines were stopped. At this point the British Light Cruiser Squadron appeared on the scene and engaged the already sinking *Mainz*, quickly reducing her to a battered hulk. Tyrwhitt then ordered a cease-fire, recalling HMS *Fearless* and her Destroyers.

Hopelessly outgunned, by the British ships, the *Mainz* had quickly succumbed and was sunk after being pounded into a smoking burning wreck. Before she sank, one of the British Destroyers, HMS *Lurcher*, went close alongside to take off survivors, of which there was around 240, only about fifty or so of which were able to walk on their own.

Following this action, one of the British Destroyers apparently became separated from sight from the remainder of the force in the mist when another German Light Cruiser appeared and opened fire on her. The British ships soon sighted her, Flotilla Leader HMS *Fearless* and several of her Destroyers and headed towards them, with the British ships then engaging the German Light Cruiser which had appeared on HMS *Arethusa's* starboard quarter and was engaged, with the German ship firing on *Arethusa*. Within minutes the British Battlecruiser Squadron suddenly appeared out of the mist. Some aboard the British Cruisers and Destroyers got a bit of a shock for a few seconds, thinking that the Battlecruisers were German until it was firmly established that they were indeed British.

The 1st Battle Cruiser Squadron, consisting of HMS *Lion* (Flagship), HMS *Princess Royal* and HMS *Queen Mary*, had sailed at 5.00 am on Thursday 27 August to rendezvous with the Rear-Admiral in HMS *Invincible*. *Invincible*, along with HMS *New Zealand* and four supporting Destroyers operating under the designation Cruiser Force K, joined up with the 1st Battle Cruiser Squadron and the situation at 4.00 pm on the 28th was that the Flotillas were steaming with the Battlecruisers being supported by the Light Cruiser Squadron and passing through the pre-arranged rendezvous point.

Admiral Beatty in HMS *Lion* was informed that the light Flotilla's had engaged the enemy in a signal from the Commodore at 08.10 am, in an area he assumed would be the general area of the rendezvous point. He remained on station with the Battle Cruiser Squadron until 11.00 am, with the intention of providing heavy support if called upon. During this time a number of communications were received, but Beatty determined that none contained any information on which he was able to act. The Battle Cruiser Squadron then came under Submarine attack around 11.00 am, although this was unsuccessful, with the Battlecruisers conducting a number of extremely sharp maneuvers to avoid the attacks. The four supporting destroyers then went on the offensive and conducted attacks on the Submarine.

Just after 11.00 am Beatty intercepted signals which indicated that both the Commodore (S) and Commodore (T) required assistance and he issued orders that the Light Cruiser Squadron would proceed to provide assistance to the Torpedo Boat Flotilla. A short time later a further signal was received from the Commodore (T) informing him that they were under attack by a large German Cruiser. Another signal received shortly after stated that he was "hard pressed" and issuing a formal request for assistance. Around this time a signal was received from Captain (D) of the First Flotilla with a request for assistance.

Beatty came to the conclusion that the situation was critical due to a number of pieces of information, including that the Flotilla's had "advanced only ten miles since 8.00 am" and also that they were in a position of only around 25 miles from two German bases - one on their flank and another one in the rear. Furthermore, the Light Cruiser Squadron was weakened due to a pair of the Light Cruisers having been released earlier in the morning to go to the assistance of some British Destroyers. (These two Light Cruisers eventually rejoined the squadron at 2.30 pm). His interpretation of reports he received was that there was a large number of German warships in the area, one of which he thought was a large Cruiser. He therefore came to the conclusion that the light forces already deployed may not be strong enough to deal with the German warships; at least not rapidly enough, leaving a risk of further German reinforcements arriving. Deciding to intervene with his Battlecruisers Beatty ordered his force to alter course to East South East and worked the Battlecruisers up to full speed to close the distance in order to provide overwhelming support at the highest possible speed. The high speed would reduce the risk of attack from enemy Submarines as well as increasing his opportunity to deal with the German Cruisers before any larger Battle Fleet assets could intervene if this was the enemy's intention. As well as the high speed of his force, attack by enemy Submarines was all the more difficult due to the flat nature of the sea, which would make spotting and identification of a Submarine periscope relatively easy.

Beatty calculated that his force of Battlecruisers was powerful enough to deal with any German force with the exception of a Battle squadron of Dreadnought Battleships. He further calculated that a clash with a German Battle Squadron was unlikely, particularly if his stroke against the German Cruisers was done quickly, as the slow speed of the German Battleships would preclude them from reaching the area fast enough unless they had already been at sea in the vicinity and he had no reports to suggest this. Furthermore, the high speed of his Battlecruisers would have allowed him to retire and avoid a full confrontation with a Battle Squadron if one had been sighted.

Beatty sighted the *Active Class* Scout Cruiser HMS *Fearless* and the 1st Flotilla retiring to the west at 12.15 pm and at the same time the British Light Cruiser Squadron was spotted to his front engaging a German Warship. Observing that the British Cruisers apparently had the German Warship defeated Beatty steered a course to the North East heading for the sounds of further gunfire now to his front. At 12.30 pm the Light Cruiser HMS *Arethusa* and the 3rd Flotilla were observed on a westward course while involved in an engagement with the German Cruiser, Beatty identified as of the *Kolberg* Class, on his port bow. Beatty then moved to position himself to cut the Cruiser off from its route to base in the Heligoland and then HMS *Lion* opened fire on her at 12.37 pm. The German Cruiser altered course North East at 12.42 and Beatty gave chase at a speed of 27 knots. At 12.56 am he observed a two-funnel Cruiser and HMS *Lion* commenced firing on the target, getting off two salvoes at her before she was enveloped in the north sea mist; Beatty noting that she had been hit by a number of heavy shells and was "burning furiously and in a sinking condition."

As he had received reports from Destroyers of mines to the eastward, Beatty decided not to follow the German Cruiser into the mist due to the risks. He, therefore, ordered his Battlecruisers to retire north, circling to port in order to re-engage the first German ship the *Lion* had engaged. This vessel was re-sighted at 1.25 pm on a South East course. HMS *Lion* engaged her with two main battery turrets firing two salvoes, following which the German ship sank.

He then dispatched four Destroyers to search the area for survivors, but unfortunately none were found.

Following the appearance of Beatty's Battlecruisers *Arethusa* then proceeded homeward with 9 Destroyers of the First Flotilla and 14 of the Third Flotilla. Having suffered much damage in the various engagements, *Arethusa's* speed was reduced to only 6 knots, and by 7.00 pm it was apparent that she was not able to continue under her own steam. All but two of her boilers were dampened as she called for assistance, eventually being taken under tow by HMS *Hogue* (Captain Wilmot S Nicholson) at 9.30 pm, under conditions of almost complete darkness. Hogue towed *Arethusa* to the Nore, where she arrived at 5.00 pm on the 29th. By this time she could raise steam for very slow speed enabling her to continue to Chatham under her own power.

Beatty ordered his Battlecruisers onto a northward course at 1.40 pm, following which HMS *Queen Mary* was attacked by a Submarine, with the Torpedo avoided "by the use of the helm." HMS *Lowestoft* was also subjected to Submarine attack but avoided the Torpedoes. Beatty's Battlecruisers then covered the retirement of the British force until all Destroyers and Light forces were accounted for by 6.00 pm. He then spread his Light Cruisers and conducted his sweep northward. HMS *Liverpool* was detached from the force and sent to Rosyth with 86 German prisoners (the survivors from the *Mainz*).

Campbell's Cruiser Force moved eastward and met up with four other Destroyers, including HMS *Lurcher*, which was escorting the Destroyers HMS *Laurel* and *Liberty* until these ships reached Campbell's Cruiser Force. HMS *Laurel*, commanded by Engineer Lieutenant-Commander Edward H. T. Meeson, had suffered serious damage when some of her own Lyddite exploded, almost completely demolishing her after funnel. Following this incident the ship retired from the action under her own steam.

At 4.30 pm on 28 August the wounded prisoners were to HMS *Bucchante* and HMS *Cressy* by boat, with these vessels then leaving for the Nore. HMS *Laurel* was taken in tow by HMS *Amethyst*. At 9.30 pm HMS *Hogue* had been detached from Campbell's Cruiser in order to take HMS *Arethusa* in tow.

From HMS *New Zealand*

When firing from the Light Cruiser Squadron was noted about eight miles distant on the port bow of HMS *New Zealand*, speed was ordered increased to maximum on course S.E. *New Zealand* was in the Van of the Battle Cruiser Squadron line. As the distance closed flashes from guns could be made out through the mist, off to the left of the position of the Light Cruiser Squadron. At this time, HMS *Arethusa*, in company with her Destroyers, passed on *New Zealand's* port side, obviously returning from the enemy, who were still firing on the British ships, with projectiles landing amongst the *Arethusa* and Destroyers.

HMS *Lion* opened fire "on something" off her port bows, but no target, only flashes from guns firing, could be observed from the *New Zealand* through the thick mist made worse by smoke. It was noted that a few enemy shells landed near HMS *New Zealand*, causing splashes some 20 ft high when they burst in the water.

HMS *Queen Mary* opened fire shortly after HMS *Lion*; it being assumed that she was engaging the same target as *Lion*. The coning tower on New Zealand then reported "enemy bearing port 30", followed by the 'A' forward turret opening fire. This fire was being directed at flashes that could be made out through the mist; firing being conducted over open sight at the targets some 8,000 yards distant. As it was determined that *New Zealand's* shells were falling over the target, range was reduced to 6,000 yards, but the target was lost in the mist.

The foremast of an enemy ship was noted extending through the mist "bearing port 40". A short time later, the vessel emerged from the mist; a three funnel Light Cruiser, which immediately opened fire on HMS *New Zealand* and Princess Royal. A number of shells fell ahead of the *New Zealand*; some fell short while at least one is described as having passed in the space between the fore bridge and fore top. Although the order had been issued for New Zealand to open fire, 'Q' and 'X' turrets could not be brought to bear, and it was noted that 'A' and 'P' turrets were slow in opening fire. Shells from the *New Zealand* fell over and on the same line as the stem, the second salvo missed, but a hit was recorded with the third salvo, after which "Independent" fire was ordered.

Around this time the German vessel was apparently steering a course parallel to that of the *New Zealand*. During this engagement, reports emanating from 'Q' and 'X' turrets reported gun flashes from another vessel on a bearing of around "port 60".

As the range closed with the German Light Cruiser, she came into full view. Firing from New Zealand was intense and a shot apparently removed the enemy foremast, which brought the flag down. Not long after all of *New Zealand's* turrets had commenced firing, a sudden reduction on the targets speed threw out the deflection considerably. The reduction in the enemy's speed was thought to have been from a hit from a torpedo apparently fired from HMS *New Zealand* at 13.00 hours, with claims that this hit amidships, throwing up a vast column of water and black smoke. Following a number of misses, *New Zealand's* guns again found the target, before cease fire was ordered. By this time the enemy's guns had been silenced, the most persistent of which, the foremost one, apparently being blown overboard. The after guns of the German ship may well not have been silenced, but were unable to bear as nothing could be seen though the smoke and mist.

The German ship, identified as SMS *Koln* apparently sank quickly, her bow resting on the bottom for some time before she finally slid beneath the waves.

During the battle HMS New Zealand fired 84 (80 capped common shell and 4 armour piercing, these latter from 'A' turret) 12 inch shells. The breakdown for the New Zealand was: 'A' Turret 17 rounds from each gun (some document state 36 from this turret); 'P' Turret, 5 rounds from the right hand gun and 14 from the left hand gun; 'Q' Turret 9 rounds from right gun and 10 from the left gun; 'X' Turret 8 rounds from the right gun and 3 from the left gun. These figures correspond to 83 rounds fired, while other documents claim 84 rounds were fired as noted above.

Information from German Records

About 9.00 am on the morning of 28 August, the German Fleet received the first wireless signals from its patrols "In squares 142 and 121 enemy cruisers and destroyers are chasing 5th Flotilla." These positions were some 20 or so sea miles to the north-west of Heligoland. Following receipt of these reports the Light Cruisers SMS *Stettin* and *Frauenlob* were dispatched to assist the 5th Flotilla. Due to the tide state at the bar of the outer Jade, the earliest the German Battle Cruisers could be expected to put to sea was estimated at 1.00 pm.

At various times during the action a total of seven German Light Cruisers, SMS *Mainz, Strassburg, Koln, Stralsund, Ariadne, Kolberg* and *Danzig* were involved, along with Destroyer Flotillas I and V and two Minesweeper Divisions. SMS *Mainz* and *Koln* were sunk by British Battlecruisers, and the *Ariadne* was also sunk along with Torpedo Boat Destroyer *V187*, leader of Flotilla I. The Light Cruisers SMS *Stralsund* and *Danzig* rescued most of the surviving crew of *Ariadne*. The Light Cruisers *SMS Strassburg* and *Stettin* were both damaged, as were the Torpedo Boat Destroyers *D8, V1* and *T33*.

Information from SMS *Ariadne* action report - Captain Seebohm

On the Morning of 28 August, the German Light Cruiser SMS *Ariadne* (Harbour Flotilla of the Jade and Weser Flagship) was anchored in the Outer Jade. Around 9.00 am the sound of gunfire was heard and the *Ariadne* prepared to get under way. Soon after she received a wireless message from another Light Cruiser, SMS *Stettin* reporting that light forces at sea required support from Cruisers. *Ariadne* weighed and headed for Heligoland, joining up with the Light Cruiser SMS *Koln* (Rear-Admiral Maass flagship) in the area of the Outer Jade Lightship. The *Koln*, which was proceeding at high speed, was ahead of the *Ariadne*, with the later following more or less the same westerly course. Already at high speed, the Koln was soon out of sight, disappearing into the haze.

While heading westward, the *Ariadne* received wireless communications from the Light Cruisers SMS *Mainz* and *Strassburg*, both of which were reporting that they were engaged in action with British Destroyers. *Ariadne* headed towards the reported position of the *Mainz* and *Strassburg*, avoiding areas suspected to be mined. Picking up wireless communications, *Ariadne* understood that the *Koln* was also heading for the other Cruisers.

The *Ariadne's* first contact with British forces came around 10.00 am when a Submarine was seen on her port beam, before it submerged. Not long after this sighting the sounds of gunfire was heard coming from somewhere on the *Ariadne's* port bow and she immediately set course for that direction. The haze caused conditions of poor visibility making it difficult to see or identify other ships. Just before 2.00 pm, two ships were observed coming out through the mist on *Ariadne's* starboard bow. There was no reply to *Ariadne's* signal and she identified her as a British Armoured Cruiser (it was actually a Battlecruiser), therefore, she turned around and headed away. The other ships was being pursued by the Battlecruiser and was identified as SMS *Koln*. Luckily for the *Koln*, the Battlecruiser switched its fire from the *Koln* to the *Ariadne*, which was very quickly hit in the forward area. This caused a fire to break out in the coal bunker resulting in the stokehold being evacuated due to smoke. With five of her boilers out of commission *Ariadne's* speed was reduced to only 15 knots maximum.

The *Ariadne* soon observed another Battlecruiser following the lead ship and this ship also opened fire on the German Cruiser at ranges between 45 to 60 hm, with the firing lasting around 30 minutes or so. The German report states that the Battlecruiser may have engaged her from ranges as low as 33 hm, although it states that this is only an estimate as by this time her recording instruments were either damaged or destroyed.

The concentrated fire from the Battlecruisers began to tell with the *Ariadne* receiving "many hits from heavy guns." This included a number of hits resulting in the rear of the ship being engulfed in fire as she was hit a number of times in the forward sections of the ship. One of these shells penetrated the Cruisers armoured deck, knocking out the torpedo station. Another shell destroyed the ships sick bay. The *Ariadne's* report states that there was very little damage done to the bridge or amidships section of the ship.

As well as the many hits inflicted on the *Ariadne*, a number of shells were reported to have passed through the ships rigging, and as the Cruiser fled, presenting her rear on profile, a number of salvoes landed in the water on her port and starboard sides. The German report points out that many of the British shells failed to explode and that there were sometimes long pauses between the salvoes. Before too long, much of the crew berthing areas fore and aft were on fire. The fires were so serious that attempts to extinguish them proved fruitless and sometimes impossible as the fire-fighting equipment was destroyed in many areas.

The *Ariadne's* situation was indeed dire, but at 2.30 pm she reported that the British Battlecruisers had turned onto a westerly course. They had actually lost her in the mist. During the action some of the *Ariadne's* guns were put out of action or outright destroyed. The guns remaining in commission had to be fired under independent control as early in the action communications between the guns and fire control was knocked out.

After escaping the British Battlecruisers the crew of the *Ariadne* tried to put the fires out, although this proved to be impossible as the aft area of the ship was unable to be reached and there was much wreckage forward. The forward magazine was ordered flooded, although it was later determined that the magazine was already under water by this time. The aft magazine could not be flooded as it proved impossible to reach it. Some of the crew was trapped in areas of the ship unable to be reached due to damage such as bent deck plates. Although the forward boiler room had suffered damage, the aft boiler room and engine compartment remained undamaged and the ships rudder still worked, but her telegraph communications were knocked out, probably by a shell exploding under the conning-tower.

Conditions on the ship were now atrocious and the heat and fires began to cook off some of the ships own ammunition, although this did little damage, but scattered splinters all over, including some which pierced through to the floor of the bridge. The order was given for the crew to assemble on the focsle and the wounded were brought up on deck.

Shortly before 3.00 pm the Light Cruiser SMS *Danzig* (commanded by Captain Reiss) appeared, sending her boats to the *Ariadne*, while *Ariadne's* own cutters were lowered from amidships, which had remained relatively unscathed. Another Light Cruiser, SMS *Stralsund* (commanded by Captain Harder) soon appeared and some of the *Ariadne's* crew went to her. With crew taken off the Captain of the *Ariadne* also went to the *Stralsund* with the plan of requesting the Stralsund to take the *Ariadne* under tow, but just at this time the *Ariadne* quite suddenly healed to port and then capsized to starboard. She did not sink immediately and her keel remained above water for some time before she eventually sank beneath the waves.

As a result of the Battle of Heligoland Bight, the Germans were fully aware of the inadequacies of their defenses and the vulnerability of their light forces on patrol lines, particularly if surprised in poor weather conditions offering bad visibility. Ill able to afford the losses, particularly in Light Cruisers, the Germans began employing armed fishing trawlers on their patrol lines and by mid-September had put in place two minefields to the west of Heligoland, to increase the chances of the patrol craft safely retiring if threatened by British forces.

1st Battle Cruiser Squadron
HMS *Lion*
HMS *Princess Royal*
HMS *Queen Mary*

Cruiser Force K
HMS *Invincible*
HMS *New Zealand*

1st Light Cruiser Squadron

Flotilla Leaders - HMS *Arethusa* and HMS *Fearless*. In addition to these major units the British Force also included the Destroyer and Submarines

German Light Cruisers

SMS Koln (*Kolberg* Class) - weight around 4,350 tons, speed 27 knots, 12 x 10.5-cm guns - sunk
SMS *Mainz* (*Kolberg* Class) - 4,400 tons, 27 knots, 12 x 10.5-cm guns - sunk
SMS *Frauenlob* (*Gazelle* Class), around 2,700 - 3,000 tons, 21.5 knots, 10 x 10-5-cm guns, 2 x 45-cm torpedo tubes
SMS *Ariadne* (Gazelle Class) - sunk
SMS *Stettin* (*Konigsberg* Class) 3,400-3,800 tons, 24.1 knots, 10 x 4.1-in (10.5-cm) guns, 2 x 18-in (45-cm) torpedo tubes
In addition to the Light Cruisers sunk, the Torpedo Boat *V187* was also sunk

The British Destroyer HMS *Lurcher* stands by as SMS *Mainz* sinks at the Battle of Heligoland Bight.

Following its successful action against the German Light Forces the previous day, the 1st Battle Cruiser Squadron, accompanied by the 1st Light Cruiser Squadron (minus *HMS Liverpool*, which was detached from the Squadron to take prisoners to be landed at Rosyth), arrived at Scapa Flow at 7.00 pm on 29 August, where it commenced refueling.

The Admiralty had received information that a mine-laying operation was planned by the Germans in an area off either the Moray or the Pentland Firth on the night of 31 August/1 September 1914. Consequently, on 31 August the Commander-in-Chief ordered all vessels either at sea or ready for sea to conduct sweeps towards the Scottish mainland coast, with the aim of intercepting the enemy minelayers on their return voyage to their base areas on the German North Sea Coast. The main elements utilised in this sweep operation were the 1st Battle Cruiser Squadron, the 3rd Battle Squadron and the 3rd and 10th Cruiser Squadrons. The information, however, had proved inaccurate and no mine laying took place, resulting in an unproductive sweep.

From 1 to 5 September, the main Battle Fleet was cruising back and forth in an area from the North-East coast of Scotland to an area just off Norway. The Cruiser Squadrons, including the 1st Battle Cruiser Squadron, were conducting sweeps further southward during this time, before joining the main Battle Fleet at sea on 3 September to begin a series of fleet exercises. During this period the strength of the 1st Battle Cruiser Squadron had been increased with the addition of *HMS Inflexible*, which had returned from the Mediterranean. This meant the 1st Battle Cruiser Squadron now had a nominal strength of five Battlecruisers: *HMS Lion* (Flagship), *Princess Royal, Queen Mary, New Zealand and Inflexible.*

On 3 September that the Admiralty received reports indicating that German Cruisers possibly intended to enter into the North Sea proper, passing through the Skagerrak (Jutland Bank). To counter to this Jellicoe ordered a sweep towards the entrance of the Skagerrak by the 1st Light Cruiser Squadron and the 2nd and 3rd Cruisers Squadrons, with the 1st Battle Cruiser Squadron as heavy support, screened by the 2nd Destroyer Flotilla. The sweep commenced from Latitude 58 N., Longitude 2.38 E., at 4.00 am on 4 September, with the aim of arriving off the entrance to the Skagerrak sometime before noon that day.

From this point the 1st Light Cruiser Squadron and the 2nd Destroyer Flotilla began a further sweep from the Skagerrak on a wide frontal area on the Ekersund-Pentland Line towards the Pentland Firth. This was probably due to the conclusion being drawn that German Submarines were operating in the Ekersund-Pentland Line. It was hoped that Submarines would be intercepted on the Surface during the hours of darkness. At the end of the sweep the 1st Light Cruiser Squadron was to make for Scapa for refueling, while the 2nd Flotilla would proceed westward of the Orkney Islands to conduct a sweep for German Submarines before making for Longthorpe, where they arrived at 9.00 pm on 6 September. Meanwhile, the 1st Battle Cruiser Squadron and the 2nd and 3rd Cruiser Squadrons cruised to the southward of the Skagerrak for a time before moving North on the return, with the 1st Battle Cruiser Squadron proceeding to Rosyth and the 2nd and 3rd Cruiser Squadrons making for Cromarty. Immediately following this operation the 4th Destroyer Flotilla was ordered to make another sweep of the Ekersund-Pentland line looking for German Submarine activity before returning to Longthorpe.

At 6.00 am on 7 September, the Dreadnought elements of the Battle Fleet departed Loch Ewe for exercises, minus HMS *Orion*, which remained as work was being carried out on her condensers. She rejoined the Battle Fleet two days later, following a 21-day hiatus from the fleet. The new Battleship, HMS *Agincourt* took her place with the 4th Battle Squadron while at sea on the 7th as she worked up with the fleet.

The Battle Fleet proceeded northward on its cruise into the North Sea passing via the Fair Island Channel somewhere around 10.00 pm on 7 September. The pre-Dreadnoughts of the 3rd Battle Squadron joined the Dreadnought Battle Squadrons around 4.00 am on 8 September.

The Battlecruisers of the 1st Battle Cruiser Squadron departed from Rosyth on the Forth just after darkness fell on 7 September and set course north-eastward and rendezvoused with the old *Apollo Class* Cruiser HMS *Sappho*, accompanied by four Destroyers of the 4th Flotilla, at 4.00 am on 8 September. These units would conduct stop and boarding duties against merchant vessels encountered as it was considered the risk of Submarine attack against a stopped ship in the North Sea was too great to risk the Battlecruisers being stopped.

The 1st Battle Cruiser Squadron conducted a sweep in a south-easterly direction in Area 6 throughout daylight hours of 8 September before moving to patrol the area from Latitude 55., Longitude 2 E., to Latitude 56.20 N., Longitude 2.40 E, where it cruised throughout the night of 8 September and into the morning of the 9th. The patrol line was chosen so as to enable the force to intercept any mine laying craft that the Germans might send out.

As the 1st Battle Cruiser Squadron and the accompanying light forces were conducting their sweep operations on the 8th, the Battleships of the Battle Squadrons remained to the eastward of the Orkney Islands conducting a series of battle tactics and gunnery practice exercises. When darkness fell on 8 September the Battle Fleet altered course heading southward to provide heavy support for a naval sweep which was to be conducted by Light forces in the Heligoland Bight on 10 September.

The sweep into Heligoland was to be conducted by the 1st and 3rd Destroyer Flotillas of the Harwich Force, with support provided by the 1st Light Cruiser Squadron and the 1st Battle Cruiser Squadron of the Grand Fleet lying to the northward and the ships of the 7th Cruiser Squadron lying to the westward. The sweep by the light forces was conducted from east to west starting an hour before dawn on 10 September, with the start point in an area between 10 and 12 miles from Heligoland. As an insurance against the unlikely emergence of the German High Seas Fleet the British Battle Fleet lay in support, covered by the 2nd and 3rd Cruiser Squadrons, occupying positions in a line some 20 miles ahead of the Battle Squadrons, which by 8.00 am on 10 September were in position Latitude 55.9 N., Longitude 4.24 E., steaming a south-south-east course at a speed of 12 knots.

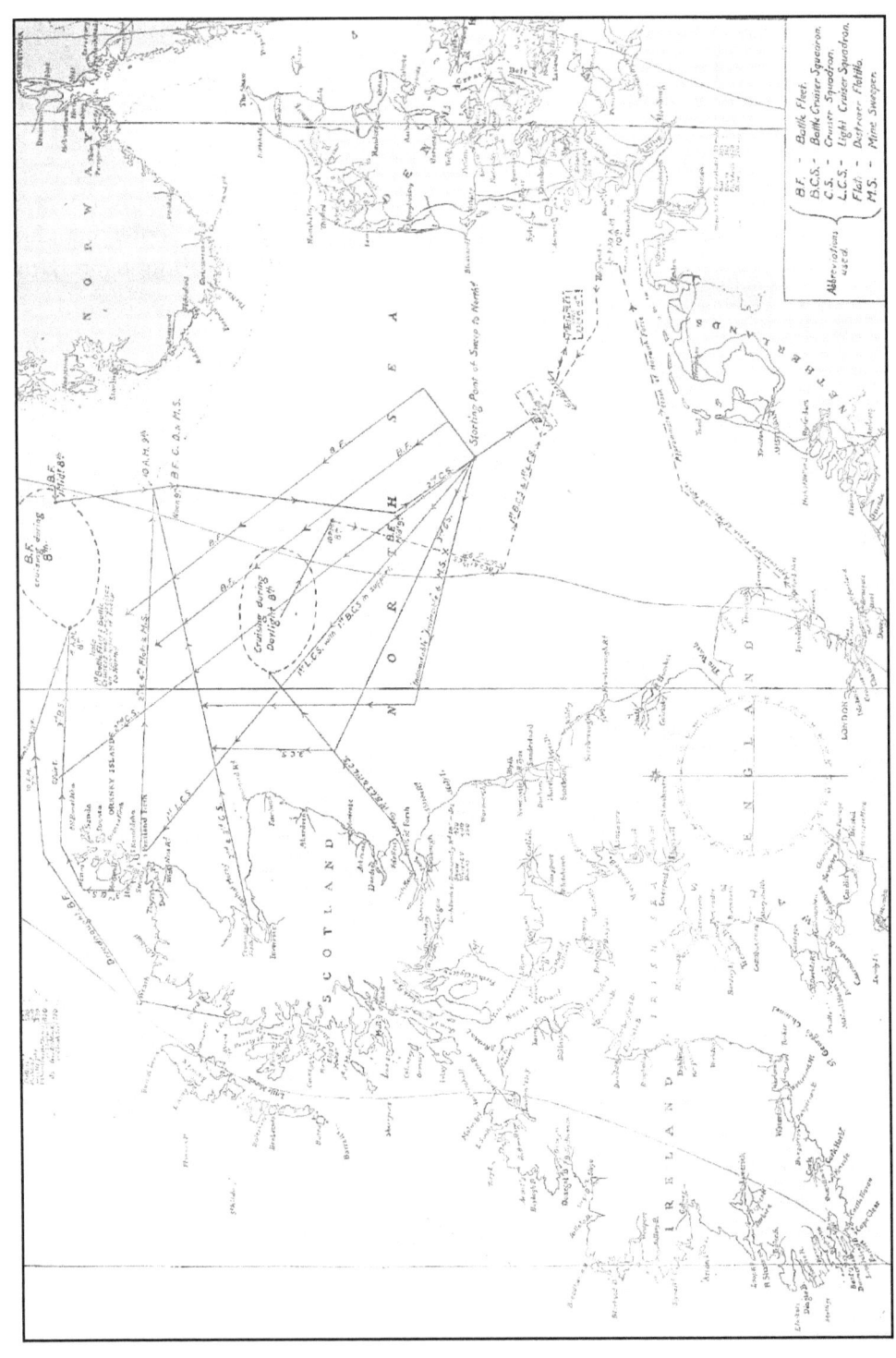

Chart showing the Grand Fleet sweep of 8 to 11 September 1914. Admiralty

The Battle Fleet and the Cruiser screen steamed in an area north-westward of Heligoland until 11.00 am, by which time the only sign of enemy activity was a seaplane sighting by the 7th Cruiser Squadron.

Following the sweep the Destroyers of the 2nd Flotilla joined the Battle Fleet to provide an anti-Submarine screen, as well as provide light forces for boarding any vessels encountered. For this latter role the 4th Destroyer Flotilla, which previously had been operating with the 2nd and 3rd Cruiser Squadrons, was ordered to join the Battle Fleet sometime during the morning of 10 September, although poor weather conditions delayed this until 2.00 pm. Bad weather had been a factor in the Heligoland Bight all that morning and had the High Seas Fleet come out with its Battle Fleet and Battle Cruisers supported by large numbers of Destroyers, some elements of the British Fleet could have been in a sticky situation, particularly as the 4th Flotilla had been so long delayed (around eight hours) in joining with the Battle Squadrons. That said the bad weather that day saw visibility drop to between 2 and 5 miles, making a successful fleet action unlikely for any side.

With the sweep of the Heligoland Bight over Jellicoe ordered a further sweep heading northward in the hope that any German ships at sea in these areas would be intercepted, as well as conducting boarding of any Fishing Trawlers and Merchant ships which were encountered.

The Battlecruisers HMS *Invincible* and *Inflexible* (operating independently of the 1st Battle Cruiser Squadron) were to conduct a sweep in a direction towards Dundee, while the 3rd Cruiser Squadron swept an area towards Aberdeen, proceeding at 12 knots. The 1st Light Cruiser Squadron swept in the direction of the Pentland Firth at 11 knots, while the 2nd Cruiser Squadron swept towards Fair Island at the slightly slower speed of 10 knots.

The 1st Battle Cruiser Squadron, with HMS *Lion* as Flagship, and also including HMS *New Zealand,* again were to be available in support of the sweeps. The Battle Fleet moved to provide a sweep screen to the eastward with each of the divisions spread at distances of around 4 miles. At 3.00 am, Jellicoe ordered the sweep to turn to N. 16 E., while some time after this the 2nd Cruiser Squadron was detached to enter into Area 7, which lay between Latitude 55.20 N. and 57.30 N., off the coast at ranges from 50 to 150 miles.

With the sweep over, the 1st Battle Cruiser Squadron and the 1st Light Cruiser Squadron joined the Battle Fleet, while the *Invincible* and *Inflexible* were dispatched to Scapa Flow in order to coal, along with the 3rd Battle Squadron, screened by a half Flotilla of Destroyers.

The 1st Battle Cruiser Squadron conducted a series of battle tactics and gunnery exercises with the Battle Fleet during 11 and 12 September, following which the Battle Fleet returned to Loch Ewe, arriving there around 5.00 pm on the 13th, while the 1st Battle Cruiser Squadron and the 1st Light Cruiser Squadron proceeded to Scapa Flow to refuel.

The Battle Fleet remained at Loch Ewe until 6.00 pm on 17 September, while the 1st Battle Cruiser Squadron remained at Scapa until the 18th. The *Inflexible* and *Invincible*, which were detached from the 1st Battle Cruiser Squadron, departed Scapa Flow during the morning of 14 September to provide heavy support for Cruiser Sweeps into Areas 3, 6 and 7 of the North Sea, which were being conducted by the 2nd 3rd, 6th and 10th Cruiser Squadrons and the Minelayer Squadron. While these operations were ongoing, a patrol was maintained eastward of the Shetlands by the Armed Merchant Cruisers *Alsatian* and *Mantua*.

When the Battle Fleet departed Loch Ewe on 17 September the new Battleship HMS *Erin* was with the Fleet for the first time. This vessel had been compulsorily purchased from Turkey, for whom it had been building, after the outbreak of war. Following gunnery firing practice to the west of the Orkneys the Battle Fleet set course through the Fair Island Channel for the North Sea, reaching position Latitude 59.23 N., Longitude 1.13 W., on a southerly course by midnight on the 18th.

After dark on the 19th, the 1st Battle Cruiser Squadron departed Scapa accompanied by the 1st Light Cruiser Squadron. Around the same time the 2nd Cruiser Squadron weighed from Cromarty and both forces moved southward to conduct a sweep of the Heligoland Bight, with the Battle Fleet positioned to provide heavy support should it be required. One of the major aims of this sweep was to conduct inspections of any trawlers sighted as there was suspicion that some were being utilised as 'look-out' vessels for the German Fleet.

The 2nd Cruiser Squadron joined with the Battle Fleet, which was in position Latitude 58.8 N., Longitude 3.20 E., by 8.00 am. The 4th Destroyer Flotilla had departed Scapa Flow and was scheduled to join-up with the 1st Battle Cruiser Squadron, while the 2nd Flotilla was due to join the Battle Fleet, but both were ordered back to Scapa due to bad weather.

The 1st Battle Cruiser Squadron now moved towards the Norwegian Coast in order to intercept and inspect Trawlers in the general area around the 'Little Fisher Bank.' While the Battle Fleet sailed behind in support, before it turned southward to meet the 3rd Battle Squadron, which had left Scapa on the 20th after coaling.

The position of the 1st Battle Cruiser Squadron at 06.20 am was Latitude 55.16 N., Longitude 4.52 E. Deteriorating weather was now making the search of Trawlers difficult, resulting in the operation being terminated with the Battle Cruisers and the Battle Fleet turning northward for home.

While the main operation was being conducted with the Battle Cruisers and Battle Fleet, the 3rd Cruiser Squadron was conducting patrols in Area 7, while the 10th Cruiser Squadron patrolled Area 6, with the *Alsatian* and *Mantua*, in company with the Armoured Cruiser HMS *Drake* from the 6th Cruiser Squadron, conducting a sweep down a stretch of the Norwegian coastline before moving to a patrol area east of the Shetlands, where they added the

Armed Merchant Cruiser *Teutonic* to their force.

As the Battle Fleet and Battlecruisers were sweeping northwards on their homeward journey Admiral Jellicoe received a wireless signal during the evening of the 21st informing him that a pair of German Light Cruisers, accompanied by Destroyers and Submarines, had been reported as having been seen from Esberg on the west coast of Denmark the previous day on a northerly course. Jellicoe ordered the fleet to turn around at midnight on the 21st and disposed his forces on a front of advance some 104 miles from the Norwegian coast out to the west into the North Sea; conducting a sweep of the area on a northerly course in the hope of intercepting the German vessels. This northward sweep continued from dawn until around 10.00 am, reaching Latitude 59 N., Longitude 2.35 E.; the position noted for the Flagship HMS *Iron Duke*. The Battle Fleet and Battlecruisers were then ordered onto a course N 5` W., in the direction of the Shetland and Orkney Islands, passing westward of the latter Island group at night on the 22nd. An attempt at gunnery practice by the Dreadnoughts of the Battle Fleet and Battlecruisers on the 23rd was abandoned due to inclement weather and the force returned to Scapa Flow on the 24th to refuel.

The Battlecruisers of the 1st Battle Cruiser Squadron weighed from Scapa Flow during the morning of the 26th on a course for the Norwegian Coast, conducting a sweep down the coast to the Naze, hoping to intercept any enemy vessels in the area. The German merchant vessel ss *Prinz Friedrich Wilhelm* had been reported as preparing to depart the Norwegian Port of Bergen. A secondary task for the Battlecruisers was to provide support for the *Drake* Class Armoured Cruiser, HMS *Drake*, the Light Cruisers HMS *Nottingham* and *Falmouth* and two Destroyers, which had been dispatched to the area to rendezvous with the two *E* Class Submarines HMS *E.1* and *E.5*, which had been conducting reconnaissance of the Skagerrak (Jutland Bank) and Kattegat in search of German ships.

On the 28th, HMS *Princess Royal* was detached from the 1st Battle Cruiser Squadron and steamed for Scapa Flow to take on fuel before continuing on to intercept and escort a convoy of Canadian Troops bound for the UK. Around this time, HMS *Invincible* and HMS *Inflexible* had been patrolling the area to the North of the Faroe Islands before sailing to meet the 1st Battle Cruiser Squadron at sea on the 29th.

At the start of October 1914, HMS *Invincible*, *Inflexible* and the 1st Battle Cruiser Squadron were at Scapa. HMS *Princess Royal* was at this time undergoing boiler cleaning in preparation for a transatlantic voyage to Halifax, Canada.

The Dreadought element of the Battle Fleet departed Scapa Flow at 5.00 pm on 2 October, followed on the morning of the 3rd by the 1st Battle Cruiser Squadron. HMS *Invincible* and *Inflexible* were now at the heart of the newly established 2nd Battle Cruiser Squadron, which departed Scapa Flow in company with the Armed Merchant Cruiser HMS *Sappho* and a trio of minelayers at 2.00

pm on the 3rd.

The bulk of the Grand Fleet was at sea by 3 October, taking up their respective pre-planned positions as the Royal Navy tightened its watch on the North Sea in order to prevent any potential break out into the North Sea and Atlantic by German Warships. The reason for this increased vigilance was part of the protection of a Canadian Troop Convoy from Halifax, Canada to the British Isles. This was the same convoy that the *Princess Royal*, along with the pre-Dreadnought Battleship HMS *Majestic*, had been sent to intercept and escort to Home Waters.

HMS *Princess Royal* was detached from the 1st Battle Cruiser Squadron for operations in the North Atlantic, where she was to meet a troop convoy crossing from Canada during the first week of October 1914. This convoy was of such political importance that the bulk of the Grand Fleet was positioned at various patrol lines to prevent a break out into the Atlantic by any significant German forces. Next page: Chart showing the approx positions of the Grand Fleet during between 3 and 11 October 1914; the period in which the Canadian troop convoy was crossing. The source of this chart is thought to be the Admiralty

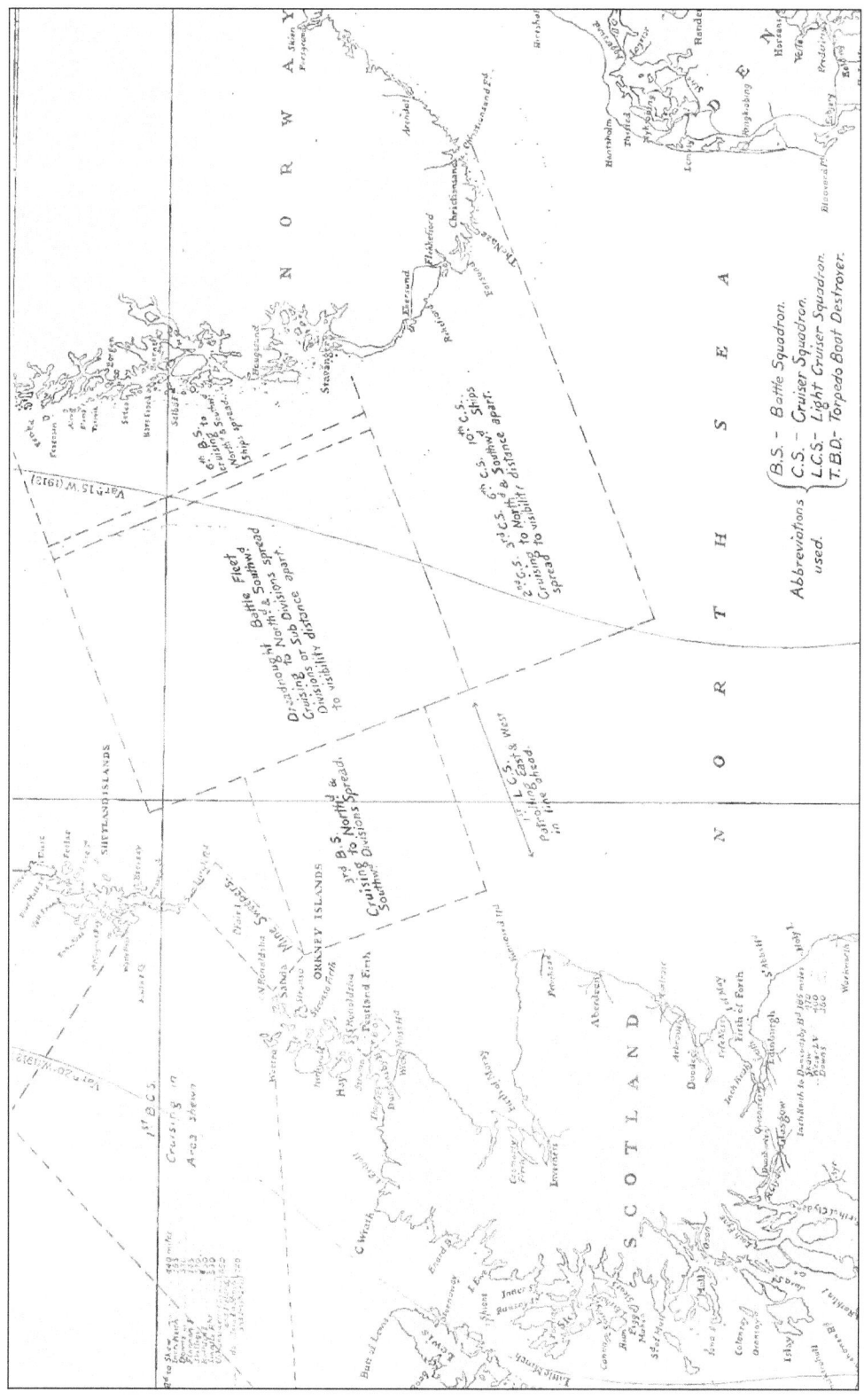

HMS *Princess Royals* planned rendezvous with the convoy did not go to plan. She arrived at the designated point in the Atlantic at 8.00 pm on 7 October, but found that the convoy was not there. It was still well to the westward, some two and a half days late.

The major effort put on by the Grand Fleet to ensure the protection of the convoy saw the major elements continually at sea or refueling between 3 and 11 October. The 1st Battle Cruiser Squadron was assigned to patrol the Fair Island Channel from its western end, while the 2nd Battle Cruiser Squadron (*Invincible* and *Inflexible*), accompanied by the Armed Merchant Cruiser *Sappho* and the three minelayers, patrolled to the eastward and northward of the Shetland Islands chain. The 1st Light Cruisers Squadron was assigned to watch the northern segment of Area 4. The 2nd and 3rd Cruiser Squadrons were watching Area 5, while the 10th Cruiser Squadron was also assigned to patrol in Area 5. The area eastward of the Fair Island Channel was patrolled by minesweepers and the Dreadnought elements of the Battle Fleet, which spread its respective Divisions on a wide area north of Area 5. The 3rd Battle Squadron patrolled northward of Area 4 and the 6th Battle Squadron was assigned to watch over the water between Norwegian territorial limits and the Dreadnought Battle Fleet.

At 5.30 pm on 12 October, the 1st Battle Cruiser Squadron accompanied by the 1st Light Cruiser Squadron departed Scapa Flow bound for the southern area of the North Sea, which was to be swept for signs of enemy shipping. From the 13th, these two Squadrons conducted a sweep on a "broad front" down towards the 'Dogger Bank', before setting course for a sweep towards the Norwegian Coast, then swinging onto a Northward course the following day. The 2nd Cruiser Squadron had joined the Battlecruisers and Light Cruisers in order to lengthen the line of the sweep on the 14th. This sweep, like so many before, proved fruitless, and on the 15th the force positioned itself to provide support to the Cruiser Squadrons that were still on patrol, while their Destroyers had been forced to head for Lerwick in order to refuel. During this time the 2nd Battle Cruiser Squadron was at Scapa.

The Cruiser Squadron patrols consisted of the 2nd and 10th Cruiser Squadrons, with the former patrolling the North East segment of Area 6, while the latter patrolled in the South Western part of Area 6. During the patrols HMS *Theseus*, an old obsolete *Edgar* Class Protected Cruiser, reported that she had been attacked by a torpedo, which had missed, in position Latitude 57.50 N., Longitude 0.33 E. This report resulted in the 10th Cruiser Squadron being withdrawn to the northern part of Area 6 before further orders, at 8.00 pm that night, saw the Squadron dispatched to join the 2nd Battle Squadron, which was steaming in an area further North.

The 10th Cruiser Squadron had lost contact with HMS *Hawke* (*Edgar* Class Protected Cruiser) and various units were ordered out from Scapa Flow to search for her; finding wreckage and survivors. The *Hawke* had been sunk by a German Submarine in latitude 57.40 N., Longitude 0.13 W., during the sweep on the 15th. As she spotted the survivors, HMS *Swift* was also attacked by a German Submarine, although the torpedoes missed.

A series of Submarine reports in Northern Waters and near Scapa Flow caused real alarm among the Grand Fleet. Admiral Jellicoe had come to the conclusion that until the anchorage could be made more secure alternative temporary bases should be used for the high value assets such as Battleships and Battlecruisers. Loch Ewe had already proved to be equally, if not more, vulnerable than Scapa Flow ruling this base out. Lough Swilly was selected as it was a defended port and the shallow waters at the entrance made it difficult for Submarines to enter undetected. However, space was a problem with so many ships requiring to be berthed, resulting in Loch-na-Keal on the Island of Mull being selected to house ships not able to berth at Lough Swilly.

Almost at once, the 1st Battle Cruiser Squadron and the 2nd Battle Squadron were ordered to Loch-na-Keal, along with the necessary Colliers and repair ships. HMS *Illustrious* (*Majestic* Class Pre-Dreadnought Battleship), which had been at Loch Ewe was also ordered to Loch-na-Keal to take up position as a guard ship.

While this was in progress the 2nd Battle Cruiser Squadron, along with the 1st and 4th Battle Squadrons, were steaming North-West of the Hebrides' as part of a blockade as well as conducting practices.

Another effect the sinking of the *Hawke* had was the withdrawal of the regular Cruiser blockade line well to the North as it was deemed that they were far too vulnerable to torpedo attack, particularly in the southern part of the North Sea. A new blockade line was therefore established to the North of the Shetland Islands. This supplemented the other blockade line formed by the Capital ships to the North-Westward of the Hebrides'.

The 2nd Battle Cruiser Squadron was ordered to Cromarty to refuel, arriving there on 21 October. That same day the Admiralty received a report that a number of German Cruisers and Destroyers had departed Danzig on 17 October, bound for the North Sea. In response to this information the 1st Battle Cruiser Squadron and 1st Light Cruiser Squadron sailed on the morning of the 21st to conduct a sweep of the North Sea on a "broad front" towards the Skagerrak. Anti-Submarine protection was provided by a screen from the 4th Destroyer Flotilla, which was forced to return to base on the 22nd due to stormy weather in the North Sea. The Battlecruisers and Light Cruisers continued the sweep towards the Skaw, before turning north and sweeping towards the Norwegian Coast. No enemy ships were sighted and the force turned for home with the 1st Battle Cruiser Squadron going to Cromarty, while the Light Cruisers went to Scapa Flow.

On 22 October, the 2nd Battle Cruiser Squadron, accompanied by four Destroyers, was temporarily detached from the Grand Fleet and sailed for the southern North Sea to join Commodore (T) supporting an operation to launch a seaplane operation in the Heligoland Bight. The Seaplane operation was cancelled due to difficulties in getting the aircraft to alight from the water and the Battlecruisers returned to Cromarty.

The Battlecruisers were at Cromarty on the 26th when Submarines were reported, although investigations found the reports to be false, but not before a major incident had unfolded as noted below:

The Battle of Jemimaville – October 1914

The incident which has come to be known under the rather spurious title The Battle of Jemimaville' was not surprisingly shrouded in a veil of secrecy during World War 1 and for many decades, thereafter, and details still remain vague almost 100 years after the incident. There was no official despatch for this action, which was a major embarrassment to the Admiralty. In late October 1914, the 1st Battle Cruiser Squadron moved to an anchorage at Invergordon in the Cromarty Firth, North Eastern Scotland. Although this anchorage was protected by some shore guns at the entrance, it was completely devoid of any submarine defenses such as nets. From Chapleton Point running south towards the anchorage there was an area of shoal water. The Battlecruisers had apparently just arrived on the 26th and dropped anchor in the anchorage when a Destroyer passed the shoal with water forced away from her bow crashing on the shoal giving an illusion of a wake left by a submarine periscope. Almost immediately one of the anchored Battlecruisers, the *Lion,* opened fire on the suspected periscope with her 4-in secondary battery. The surprise and probably shock at seeing one Battlecruiser firing on a suspected target prompted at least one other vessel to open fire. According to eyewitness, from at least one of the Battlecruisers (probably the second one to open fire), it looked as if the original bombardment was aimed at a small group of trees on the shore, from which it seemed that fire was being returned towards the ships. There was some wonderings if the Germans had landed some field guns and somehow managed to place them in the small forest unobserved. Eye witness reports stated that there was most defiantly flashes coming from the forest and smoke was certainly observed coming from the area. By this point there was a storm of 4-in gunfire being directed towards the shore, and then suddenly a flag was hoisted ordering the ships to ceasefire. As suddenly as the warships ceased-fire so too did the supposed firing from the small wood appear to stop.

It was now becoming quite clear that it was impossible for a Submarine periscope to have been sighted since the water in that area was a mere 2 or 3 feet in depth. The suspected gunfire that was coming from the small forest was nothing more than flashes of exploding 4-in shells some of which had initially ricochet from the water into the forest and then some were deliberately aimed direct into the forest as firing commenced at the suspected German guns.

With many eyes now trained on the small forest, it was soon discovered that a number of small Cottages were located within it, being on the outskirts of the Village of Jemimaville, which lay about 7 km west of Cromarty and 3 km south of Invergordon. Personnel went ashore to determine if there were any casualties. By good fortune, most of the Cottages had been just outside the area which had been subjected to the intense bombardment. Little damage had been suffered, with some roofs and brickwork, particularly to chimneys, being slightly damaged from shrapnel. There was only a single casualty, a baby, which had suffered a cut on one of its legs due to a slate falling from the roof when the roof was damaged. After apologising to the parents, the officer returned to ship, only to be dispatched to shore again.

The firing had certainly not gone un-noticed on shore to others other than the occupants of the Cottages. Stories ran wild and the local papers were drawing up sensational headline stories of the anchorage in the Cromarty Firth being under heavy attack from German Submarines. A naval party accompanied the officer to stop the stories going to press.

The baby was treated by a naval Doctor and the parents were told a terrific false tale of 2 or three German Submarines having been sunk with all hands during the Battle, which was not being admitted to have been an error. Their roof was repaired and their silence asked for and apparently received. The Admiralty no doubt wanted the incident hushed as it being made public in late 1914 would have brought the Cromarty Firth to the attention of the German Navy, which would have welcomed the news that there were no Submarine defences in place in an anchorage sometimes used by British Capital Ships.

It is indeed ironic that the much publicised bombardments of British Coastal town by German Battlecruisers from November 1914 were actually preceded by the British bombardment of Jemimaville.

During October and November 1914, the Battle Cruiser Force facing the Germans in the North Sea was probably at its weakest point of the entire war. HMS *Princess Royal*, HMS *Invincible* and HMS *Inflexible* were then operating in the Atlantic Ocean as a counter to Von Spee's Cruiser Force (Princess Royal was in the North Atlantic, the other two vessels were making for the South Atlantic), which was attempting to make it back to Germany from the Pacific. HMAS *Australia* was still en-route to Britain from the Pacific and would not arrive for some time yet and HMS *Indomitable* was still en-route from the Mediterranean, where she had left the *Indefatigable*. This left only HMS *Lion* (Flagship), HMS *Queen Mary* and HMS *New Zealand* for work in the North Sea, as the newly built HMS *Tiger* was still not ready for service.

Towards the end of October 1914, HMS *New Zealand* was undergoing dockyard work at Cromarty. This reduced the Battlecruiser force to only five available for operations. A number of Dreadnought Battleships were undergoing necessary work, due to among other things, defects with condenser tubes, which had plagued a number of ships, including the flagships *Iron Duke* and the *Orion,* for some time. It is often stated, and indeed Admiral Fishers own writings confirm this, that the effective Dreadnought elements of the Grand Fleet available at this time was only 17 Battleships and the five available Battlecruisers (HMS *New Zealand* being in dockyard hands as noted above). This being the case, the 15 Battleships and four Battlecruisers (five if the *Blucher* is counted, although this was not a true Battlecruiser, but rather an evolved modern Armoured Cruiser) meant that the Grand Fleet possessed an extremely thin margin of superiority over the German High Seas fleet. Furthermore, the Germans were known to have around 88 Destroyers and Torpedo Boat Destroyers available compared with only 42 available to the Grand Fleet. However, to a certain extent these figures are misleading as they do not include the two newly commissioned Battleships, HMS *Erin* and *Agincourt*, nor do they take into account the likelihood of some of the German Capital ships being unavailable. As regards the German superiority in Destroyers, this too was overstated, as the German Destroyers had a number of responsibilities and had to cover the North Sea coast and the Baltic. The British figure of 42 Destroyers available did not include the Harwich Force, which covered the southern North Sea and was included in the forces that would be available to the Grand Fleet in a planned Fleet action, although it would at times be difficult for the two forces to join together for such an action owing to the vast distances between their respective base areas.

The Grand Fleet was further weakened when it was decided to send the 3rd and 6th Battle Squadrons (Pre-Dreadnoughts) south to join the Channel Fleet. However, following the German bombardment of the English East Coast noted below, the 3rd Battle Squadron was returned North and based on Rosyth along with the 3rd Cruiser Squadron, with both arriving at Rosyth on 20 November. The reasoning for basing these Squadrons at Rosyth was to allow them to respond quicker to any attempt by the Germans to land an Army on the East coast of Great Britain, something which was considered a threat throughout the war. It was in the early months of the war, however, that the danger of such a landing was greatest as the British Army was extremely small in comparison with the Great European Powers, and the cream of that Army had been moved to France and Belgium leaving the British Isles very bare, while the Volunteer Army was being built up. Later in the war, the risk, which while still present, was considered far less potent as defenses and manpower had been put in place to counter invasion.

While Jellicoe was away at a conference, the Admiralty issued orders for the Grand Fleet to proceed from Lough Swilly to Scapa Flow, but these were duly cancelled when he returned to Lough Swilly around noon on 3 November, at which time he took control of the Grand Fleet again. The 1st, 2nd and 4th Battle Squadrons sailed at 3.45 pm, bound for the coast of Galloway to conduct firing practice, which was conducted the following day before the fleet sailed north.

German Bombardment of Yarmouth

On the early morning of 3 November 1914, the German Battlecruisers appeared off the east coast town of Yarmouth and conducted a bombardment aimed at inflicting damage on the harbor facilities and the town's fortifications. The bombardment doubled as a cover for mines to be laid in the area, following which the German forces withdrew, the only casualty being the Armoured Cruiser SMS *Yorck*, which after hitting a mine in misty conditions in the Jade, capsized. British forces including Battlecruisers sailed to try and catch the German raiding force, but no contact was made as the German force was too far ahead.

News had reached the Grand Fleet on 3 November that a Light Cruiser of the Harwich Force, HMS *Undaunted,* was being pursued by a number of German warships in the Southern North Sea. In addition, a further report claimed German Battlecruisers had been observed off Gorleston on the Norfolk coast. It was this claimed sighting that prompted the 3rd Battle Squadron to be ordered back North to re-join the main fleet at Scapa Flow.

The 1st and 2nd Battle Cruiser Squadrons were ordered to proceed towards Heligoland at the fastest possible speed, with the 1st Light Cruiser Squadron accompanying them. The 2nd and 6th Cruiser Squadrons were ordered to Scapa to refuel and to be ready for sea again as soon as possible, while the 10th Cruiser Squadron went to the Shetlands. All these movements of Grand Fleet assets were a counter to the possibility that the German Battlecruiser sighting was part of a "general movement", which proved not to be the case, resulting in the orders being cancelled as there would be no chance of intercepting the German warships before they returned to port.

As noted above, the *Invincible* and *Inflexible* were detached from the Grand Fleet by Admiralty orders and departed Cromarty on 5 November 1914, bound for Devonport to prepare for their journey to the South Atlantic to search for Von Spee's Cruiser Squadron, which had destroyed Admiral Cradocks Cruiser Squadron off Coronel on the 4th. This great increase of strength for British forces in the Southern Atlantic would be well justified when they engaged the German Cruiser Squadron in December 1914. However, while fully concurring with the necessity of sending the Battlecruisers South, Jellicoe was well aware that it seriously eroded the Grand Fleets superiority over the German High Seas Fleet. On the plus side, 6 November saw the arrival of the new Battlecruiser HMS *Tiger* at Scapa Flow. The *Tiger* had been conducting a series of working up voyages, which included gunnery and torpedo practice exercises in the area of Bantry Bay in southern Ireland. Her arrival at Scapa was to prepare her for further working up before she joined the 1st Battle Cruiser Squadron.

On 6 November, the 1st Battle Cruiser Squadron, 1st Light Cruiser Squadron and half of the 4th Destroyer Flotilla departed Cromarty for a sweep of the North Sea, following which the Battlecruisers and Destroyers returned to

Cromarty, while the Light Cruisers went to Scapa Flow.

On 17 November various elements of the Grand Fleet sailed to take positions designed to counter a "suspected" attempt by the High Seas Fleet to break out to the Atlantic with a the number of ships. The main units deployed included the 1st Battle Cruiser Squadron, 2nd Battle Squadron, 1st Light Cruiser Squadron and the 2nd Cruiser Squadron, with a half Destroyer Flotilla screening them. The Dreadnoughts of the 2nd Battle Squadron were deployed to the westward, while the Battlecruisers, Cruisers and Light Cruisers, with their Destroyer screen, operated to the eastward of the Shetland Islands. No enemy vessels were encountered and the Battlecruisers and Light Cruisers returned to Scapa Flow on 20 November, followed the next day by the 2nd Battle Squadron and 2nd Cruiser Squadron.

HMS *Princess Royal*, which had been detached from the Grand Fleet, departed for Halifax, Canada on 11 November 1914 to reinforce the North American Squadron as a counter to the possibility of Von Spee's Cruiser Squadron breaking out into the Caribbean and North Atlantic via the Panama Canal. Admiral Jellicoe objected to the sending of the *Princess Royal*, suggesting the older less powerful HMS *New Zealand* should be sent in her place. However, Admiralty orders remained and *Princess Royal* headed West.

It should be remembered, that at this early stage in the war there was enormous sympathy for the German cause in the United States of America, not least because she was fighting the United States natural enemy at the time; Great Britain. Although, the United States and Great Britain's relations had improved considerably since the war of 1812-14, and ensuing tensions between the two nations throughout the nineteenth Century, it was for war with Great Britain that the United States main military planning was aimed against. In the United States, crews of German vessels running the British blockade were treated as heroes and even military vessels such as Submarines were docking in American ports.

For Britain, a watchful eye had to be kept on the United States, which had a number of territorial ambitions, which at the time were British possessions, Dominions or Territories. Canada too, had to keep a watchful eye on its Southern neighbour, as the United States had long harbored plans to invade and subjugate Canada into the United States; the main reason behind the war of 1812.

There can be little doubt that the sending of the *Princess Royal* instead of the more logical choice of sending the *New Zealand* was in part to show the Americans that although faced with the threat of the German High Seas Fleet, Britain was still capable of sending powerful naval forces to other parts of the World including the North American Station. At this time, while the bulk of the fleet faced the Germans in the North Sea, the Royal Navy had two Battlecruisers in the Mediterranean, one in the North Atlantic, two heading for the South Atlantic and one in the Pacific (this latter vessel was HMAS *Australia*, which was under Admiralty control). In addition, she had a number of pre-Dreadnought Battleships and lighter forces dispersed around various theatres.

There was merit in both arguments about which vessel to send, *Princess Royal* or *New Zealand*. While, America was an unknown at the time in regards to her intentions, Britain had a very real threat in the North Sea, which included a significant threat of possible invasion. This fact alone would merit retaining the more powerful vessel in home waters, while dispatching the less powerful *New Zealand* to the North American Station. Once she was detached from the Grand Fleet HMS *Princess Royal* was away from the North Sea until early January 1915.

On 20 November 1914 the Battle Cruiser Squadron was at Scapa, lying about a mile or so from the Grand Fleet Flagship Iron Duke. The following day torpedo practice was conducted in the confines of Scapa, during the course of which one of the *Lions* torpedoes turned back towards the direction of the ship, but did not hit any vessels.

During the early evening of 22 November the Grand Fleet sailed from its respective bases to conduct a sweep of the North Sea in support of aircraft attacks on Heligoland. Almost the entire strength of the Grand Fleet was employed with the 1st, 2nd, 3rd and 4th Battle Squadrons along with the 1st Battle Cruiser Squadron and the 2nd 3rd and 6th Cruiser Squadrons, being joined by the pre-Dreadnoughts of the 3rd Battle Squadron from Rosyth. The fleet was screened by the Destroyers of the 2nd and 4th Flotillas.

The Grand fleet steamed south and was to be supported by Commodore (T) with three Light Cruisers and eight Destroyers from the Harwich Force. The main fleet was to be in position to support the air operation by dawn on the 24th. The 1st Battle Cruiser Squadron and 1st Light Cruiser Squadron had detached from the main force, along with a Division of Destroyers, during the afternoon of 23 November. This force was ordered to be in position Latitude 55.10 N., Longitude 6.20 E., at 5.30 am on the morning of the 24th.

During the course of the Night of 23/24 November, the operation was cancelled due to a suspected German force operating in the Heligoland Bight, considered superior in strength to the detached elements of the fleet scheduled to enter that area.

The opportunity was taken to attempt to draw the German force onto the main fleet and Jellicoe ordered Commodore (T) to rendezvous with the 2nd Cruiser Squadron and then sail towards Heligoland in the hope that they could draw the German warships towards the British heavy units. The Battlecruisers of the 1st Battle Cruiser Squadron, supported by the 1st Light Cruiser Squadron, were ordered to proceed towards Heligoland to provide support to the 2nd Cruiser Squadron and the Light Cruisers and Destroyers of Commodore (T).

In the Bight, the weather on the morning of the 24th was bright, offering high visibility, which aided Commodore (T) and the 2nd Cruiser Squadron in their sweep of the area. At 10.40 am Commodore (T) signaled that he could only see smoke behind the Island of Heligoland and some ships heading southward and that a Submarine had been seen. This was followed at 11.00 am when the Rear-Admiral of the 2nd Cruiser Squadron reported that he had observed a number of Destroyers, but that they would not be drawn towards him. He was, therefore, turning to the northward along with Commodore (T). Shortly after this the 1st Battle Cruiser Squadron and 1st Light Cruiser Squadron turned northward with the Battlecruisers being in position Latitude 54.47 N., Longitude 6.35 E. at noon on the 24th.

Ships of the 2nd Cruiser Squadron received the attention of an aircraft, which dropped five small bombs close to the Light Cruiser HMS *Liverpool*, which was in company with the Armoured Cruisers, at 12.35 pm.

Following a turn to the North-West at 2.00 pm, the Battle Fleet came into sight of the 1st Battle Cruiser Squadron some way astern at 3.30 pm. Dispositions for the night saw the 1st Battle Cruiser Squadron and the Light Cruisers positioned some 15 miles to the East of the main Battle Fleet.

On the 25th, a series of exercises were conducted, with the fine weather beginning to change by the afternoon, deteriorating to a southerly gale going into the morning of the 26th, resulting in the Cruisers returning to base, following the 1st Battle Cruiser Squadron, 1st Light Cruiser Squadron and the Destroyers, which had all detached from the fleet at midnight on the 25th, with the Battlecruisers going to Scapa Flow, the Light Cruisers to Rosyth and the Destroyers to Invergordon. On the 26th, the Battle Fleet abandoned its planned target practice to the north and returned to Scapa Flow arriving on the 27th.

On 1st December 1914, the new *Iron Duke* Class Battleships, HMS *Emperor of India* and HMS *Benbow* arrived at Berehaven in South Ireland for a series of working up exercises before joining the Grand Fleet. These two Battleships then sailed for Scapa to join the 4th Battle Squadron of the Grand Fleet, arriving on 10 December to work up with the fleet.

From 2 December through 6 December, there was almost continuous bad weather in the Scapa Flow area, with two severe gales during this period. No major operations were conducted during this time, although a Submarine was engaged near Holm Sound entrance and forced to dive. A sweep of the North Sea planned for the 6th was cancelled due to reports that the severe gales had dislodged a large number of sea mines from their moorings. The extremely foul weather continued with another gale on the 8th and another from the 11th to the 14th forcing most ships at sea to return to port, including the Dreadnoughts of the 1st Battle Squadron, which returned to Scapa on the 12th.

On 14 December, the 1st Battle Cruiser Squadron departed Cromarty in company with all the Destroyers which had put in there during the bad weather. The Battlecruisers and Destroyers sailed for a rendezvous with the 2nd Battle Squadron and 1st Light Cruiser Squadron, which sailed from Scapa, and the 3rd Cruiser Squadron, which sailed from Rosyth. These units were to rendezvous in approximately Latitude 57.20 N., Longitude 0.10 W., at 2.20 pm on the afternoon of 15 December, before turning onto a southward course to conduct a sweep down the western part of the North Sea. However, things did not go to plan as the 6 Battleships of the 2nd Battle Squadron (HMS *Thunderer* was absent as it was in refit) departed Scapa on the morning of the 15th, but were then forced to return to Scapa as the attached Cruisers HMS *Blanche* and *Boadicea* suffered heavy damage when they encountered very heavy seas while transiting the Pentland Firth. The *Boadicea* in particular suffered serious damage when heavy seas washed her bridge away, resulting in a number of her crew being swept overboard and drowning. *Boadicea* was detached to proceed to the River Clyde for repairs, while the *Blanche* returned to Scapa Flow.

The 1st Battle Cruiser Squadron in company with the other units was instructed to continue the sweep without the 2nd Battle Squadron. The lack of Destroyers available was causing some concern for Admiral Jellicoe, with only seven available to come out from Cromarty. To overcome the shortage available for the sweep, Jellicoe requested that the Admiralty instruct Commodore (T), together with the 1st and 3rd Destroyer Flotillas from the Harwich Force, to meet the Battlecruisers in the southern North Sea after daybreak on the 16th. However, the Harwich Force was already at sea and remained quite a distance to the south of the area being swept by the 1st Battle Cruiser Squadron and accompanying units.

The seven Destroyers out of Cromarty, HMS *Lynx, Ambuscade, Utility, Hardy, Shark, Acasta* and *Spitfire*, were stationed 10 miles in front of the 2nd Battle Squadron during the move south following the rendezvous in the Northern North Sea. These Destroyers sighted and engaged a force of German Destroyers just before Daybreak in the early morning of 16 December. The German Destroyers were apparently a forward screen for a force of a Cruiser and three Light Cruisers, which were also later engaged by the small force of seven British Destroyers.

During the course of the battle HMS *Hardy* sustained damage from enemy fire, including damage to the steering-gear and had 2 crew killed and fifteen injured. HMS *Ambuscade* and HMS *Lynx* were also hit and holed, with one of the crew of the *Lynx* being wounded. HMS *Hardy*, which claimed to have hit one of the German Light Cruisers at close range, was able to withdraw under covering fire from HMS *Lynx*. Following the engagement, the small force of British Destroyers had been scattered and each made for a variety of East Coast ports to conduct repairs and refuel, with the disabled *Hardy* being escorted into the Humber by HMS *Spitfire*.

Jellicoe did not receive a report of the engagement and had no idea that German forces were in the vicinity of the British East Coast until 08.55 am when a wireless transmission from the Admiralty to the Vice-Admiral in command of the 2nd Battle Squadron was intercepted (this message was timed 08.35 am). This was the report confirming that Scarborough on the East Coast of Northern England was being shelled by German warships.

This alarming report resulted in Jellicoe ordering the Grand Fleet to raise steam for sea, with the departure from Scapa commencing at 12.15 pm, the fleet heading for Latitude 57 N., Longitude 2.30 E. With calmer weather now in place the Destroyers were able to accompany the fleet to sea, acting as a screen. The 3rd Battle Squadron, under Vice-Admiral Bradford, based at Rosyth was also ordered to proceed to sea, weighing at 10.00 am.

The force already at sea was effectively under the command of the Vice-Admiral 2nd Battle Squadron, Sir George Warrender, who now ordered his forces to turn northward in the hope of being able to intercept the German bombardment force whilst they were on their return journey to their base. Jellicoe anticipated that the German forces would probably emerge through a gap they were known to have left from their mining operations off the British East Coast. At 10.26 am, Warrender ordered Sir David Beatty, Commander of the 1st Battle Cruiser Squadron, to pass through the gap in the minefield and close the East Coast. At 10.30 am, an Admiralty wireless message to the Commander of the 2nd Battle Squadron surmised that the German forces would already be returning to Heligoland and suggested Warrender's force should remain outside the minefield areas and instead proceed on a course to cut the Germans warships off from their base. Warrender ordered the 1st Battle Cruiser Squadron to follow these instructions, probably on the basis that their high speed meant they were the only heavy forces with a realistic chance of cutting off the enemy if he were already on his return passage to Heligoland.

The 3rd Battle Squadron from Rosyth was ordered by Jellicoe to proceed to latitude 55.50 N., Longitude 1.10 W., which would put them in a position to intercept the German force if it passed to the north of the mined areas rather than through them as was expected.

Admiral Jellicoe in his Flagship *HMS Iron Duke* received an Admiralty message stating that the Scout Patrol was under fire from two enemy Battlecruisers and that a force of German Battleships or Battlecruisers (these were Battlecruisers) were off Scarborough, whilst a force of German Light Cruisers was off Hartlepool.

The disposition of the 3rd Battle Squadron was signaled to the 2nd Battle Squadron with the 3rd Cruiser Squadron in company. The commander of the 2nd Battle Squadron signaled Jellicoe informing him that his force would be in position Latitude 54.24 N., Longitude 2.0 E. at 12.30 pm. Beatty, with the 1st Battle Cruiser Squadron and the 1st Light Cruiser Squadron, was steaming to the North-West of the 2nd Battle Squadron, while the light forces of the Harwich Force under Commodore (T) were around 60 miles to the southward on a course to take them to position Latitude 54.20 N., Longitude 1.30 E., following a signal from the commander of the 2nd Battle Squadron at 10.28 am. Conditions, whilst not very bad, were far from ideal for locating and engaging an enemy force. A North Sea mist reduced visibility to an average of around five miles.

The 1st Light Cruiser Squadron encountered the enemy at 11.30 am, when HMS *Southampton* (Commander Goodenough) reported sighting an enemy Light Cruiser and a number of Destroyers on a southerly course. The *Southampton* and HMS *Birmingham* began closing the enemy vessels and engaged them with unknown results due to the misty conditions and large amounts of spray being kicked-up over the forward part of the ships. Just before 11.50 am another three German Light Cruisers were sighted to the South-Westward of the British Light Cruisers, but contact was lost very quickly.

The 2nd Battle Squadron sighted German Destroyers and Cruisers, some five miles off to the eastward in approximately Latitude 54.23 N., Longitude 2.14 E., steaming a course of "north by west", which indicated they had emerged from the gap in the minefields as had been expected. Beatty with the 1st Battle Cruiser Squadron was still some way off, being around 15 miles to the North of the 2nd Battle Squadron. Giving all the ships positions and courses at the time and leading up to the sighting of the German force by the 2nd Battle Squadron, the German ships probably sailed a course between the 2nd Battle Squadron and the 1st Battle Cruiser Squadron. Another possibility was that it had sailed either ahead of the 2nd Battle Squadron or astern of the Battlecruisers.

On sighting the German warships, the 2nd Battle Squadron immediately altered course to try and close with the enemy, but the German ships turned to the northwards and were swallowed by the mist, evading the slower British Battleships, which were unable to engage them. Throughout the morning's events the 1st Battle Cruiser Squadron had not sighted any German Warships.

The Grand Fleet had missed an opportunity for intercepting at least part of the East Coast raiding force. Although a number of its formations were favorably placed, the low visibility offered in the misty conditions together with the absence of the Cruisers, which would normally be attached to the Battle Squadrons (this was due to adverse weather encountered in the Pentland Firth) enabled the Germans to retire without being intercepted.

Vice-Admiral Warrender of the 2nd Battle Squadron ordered the 1st Battle Cruiser Squadron and 1st Light Cruiser Squadron to reform with his squadron and the 3rd Cruiser Squadron, which at 3.00 pm were in position Latitude 54.53 N., Longitude 1.55 E., on a northward course.

Jellicoe had been informed by the Admiralty that the various direction stations information indicated the possibility that other elements of the High Seas fleet may be at sea. At 6.30 pm, Jellicoe signaled the various groups of the Grand Fleet that were at sea to make for a rendezvous at 6.00 am on the morning of the 17th. This rendezvous joined up the force which sailed from Scapa Flow, consisting of the 1st and 4th Battle Squadrons screened by the 2nd Destroyer Flotilla, the 2nd and 6th Cruiser Squadrons with Sir George Warrender's force of the 2nd Battle Squadron together with the Cruisers and Battlecruisers and the other force of the 3rd Battle Squadron commanded by Vice-Admiral Bradford and the light forces of the Harwich Force under Commodore (T), consisting of three Light Cruisers. Following this rendezvous the Grand Fleet continued on a southward course. However, any hopes of meeting any sizable element of the High Seas Fleet were dashed following a signal received during the course of the afternoon, which informed Jellicoe that new information indicated that the German ships, which had been at sea were now back in port.

With the main part of the Grand Fleet at sea Jellicoe decided to take the opportunity to conduct a series of fleet battle exercises. Just before dark, Commodore (T) with the three Light Cruisers of the Harwich Force detached from the Grand Fleet and returned to Harwich. The 3rd Battle Squadron, together with the 3rd Cruiser squadron returned to Rosyth and the 2nd Battle Squadron with the 2nd Destroyer Flotilla returned to Scapa Flow. The Battleship HMS *Marlborough* from the 1st Battle Squadron also went to Rosyth to facilitate a changeover of command between Sir Lewis Bayly and Sir Cecil Burney, as orders to this effect had been received from the Admiralty while the fleet was at sea. Vice-Admiral Burney would take command of the 1st Battle Squadron, while Sir Lewis Bayly was to take over command of the channel fleet. The *Marlborough* returned to Scapa Flow on the 21st, where Vice-Admiral Burney joined his squadron. Rosyth was also the destination of the Light Cruiser HMS *Bellona* and Flotilla Leader HMS *Broke*, which collided during the battle exercises. These two ships were escorted to Rosyth by HMS *Devonshire*.

The other elements of the fleet, consisting of the 1st and 4th Battle Squadrons, 1st Battle Cruiser Squadron, and the 1st Light Cruiser Squadron, continued cruising to the eastward of the Orkney Islands during 18 December. That evening, the 1st and 4th Battle Squadron set course to return to Scapa Flow where they arrived on 19 December, while the 1st Battle Cruiser Squadron and 1st Light Cruiser Squadron made for Cromarty, also arriving on 19 December. The 6th Cruiser Squadron continued to patrol the Northern North Sea, while the 1st and 2nd Cruiser Squadrons made for Cromarty. During the 17th, signals were received confirming that some merchant ships had been sunk by mines which were laid by the German warships of the Yorkshire coast.

The 1st Battle Cruiser Squadron, with the 1st Light Cruiser Squadron in company, departed Cromarty on 21 December bound for Rosyth following receipt of orders from the Admiralty that the Battle Cruiser Squadrons along with the 1st Light Cruiser Squadron should be stationed there. Basing the Battlecruisers at Rosyth was a direct consequence of the German raid on Scarborough as it was clear the Battlecruisers would be better placed to try and intercept future East Coast raids by being based further south than Cromarty.

The Grand Fleet maintained its dominant presence in the North Sea when the 2nd and 4th Battle Squadrons and the fleet Flagship, HMS *Iron Duke*, sailed from Scapa on 23 December, steaming to the westward of the Orkney Islands for target practice; conducted on the 24th at Sulis-Ker Rock, to the North of the Hebrides. Following this, the two Battle Squadrons sailed through the Pentland Firth around 6.00 pm and entered the North Sea to begin a sweep to the South.

This planned sweep saw the 1st Battle Squadron in company with the 2nd Destroyer Flotilla and 6th Cruiser Squadron depart from Scapa, while the 1st Battle Cruiser Squadron, 1st Light Cruiser Squadron, 3rd Battle Squadron and 3rd Cruiser Squadron left Rosyth during the course the 25th. The 1st and 2nd Cruiser Squadrons and the 4th Destroyer Flotilla left Cromarty on the 25th, with all forces to rendezvous with the flagship, *Iron Duke's,* force in an area between Latitude 56.45 N., Longitude 1.30 E., and Latitude 56.14 N., Longitude 3.20 E, with the fleet having effectively joined up by 1.20 pm on the 25th. Course was set for South-South-East with the fleet proceeding at a speed of 15 knots.

HMS Birmingham and *HMS Southampton* from the 1st Light Cruiser Squadron reported Submarine sightings some 15 miles south westward of the main Battle Fleet at 1.40 pm. Following this, the Battle Fleet gradually changed course until it was steaming North-North-Eastward by 3.00pm on the 25th. Another change of course was ordered and the fleet turned to North-North-West at 3.15 pm, and reduced speed. The fleet turned onto a southward course at 9.15 pm, but was forced to reduce speed further as heavy seas were taking their toll on the Destroyers. The weather worsened as the night wore on until by midnight the winds were at gale force.

The bad weather continued throughout the night and worsened by morning. The position of the Battle Fleet at 8.00 am on Boxing Day was Latitude 55.58 N., Longitude 2.16 E., and the Battlecruisers and the 1st Light Cruiser Squadron were located some 40 miles to the south. The heavy weather was making the going extremely difficult for the Destroyers, with 11 knots the best speed that they could expect to attain without risking being seriously damaged. The going for the smaller vessels was proving too difficult and Jellicoe ordered the Destroyers to make for their bases at 8.10 am on the 26th.

The heavy weather eventually led to the sweep being abandoned and the fleet turned onto a northward heading. At 11.00 am the various elements of the fleet were ordered to detach and return to their respective bases, with the Battle Fleet heading for Scapa, while the other elements returned to Cromarty and Rosyth. The *Invincible Class* Battlecruiser *HMS Indomitable* had joined the fleet at sea at 8.00 am on the 26th, following her passage from the Mediterranean and this vessel was ordered to make for Rosyth and join the 1st Battle Cruiser Squadron.

The Grand Fleet attained an additional Light Cruiser Squadron, when the 2nd Light Cruiser Squadron consisting of HMS *Falmouth* (Squadron Flagship under Rear-Admiral Trevelyan), HMS *Gloucester,* HMS *Yarmouth* and HMS *Dartmouth* was formed on 28 December 1914.

5

THE BATTLE OF THE FALKLAND ISLANDS

HMS *Invincible* and *Inflexible* were detached from the Grand Fleet by Admiralty orders and departed Cromarty on 5 November 1914, bound for Devonport to prepare for their journey to the South Atlantic to search for Von Spee's Cruiser Squadron, which had destroyed Admiral Cradock's Cruiser Squadron off Coronel on the 1 November; the Armoured Cruisers HMS *Good Hope* (Rear Admiral Cradocks Flagship) and *Monmouth* both being sunk. The Light Cruiser HMS *Glasgow* and the Armed Merchant Cruiser HMS *Otranto* escaped.

Lord Fisher's letters claim that he was informed that HMS "*Invincible* or *Inflexible*" would not be able to leave Devonport for some two days later than the designated date due to "some defect in the brickwork of her boilers." However, Fisher insisted and they left on the designated date.

Invincible departed from Devonport bound for St Vincent where she took on coal. She then sailed for the coast of South America, bound for the Abrolhos Islands to again coal. Nine Colliers and a pair of oil ships had been positioned at Abrolhos to replenish the British Squadron which was assembling there.

The powerful South Pacific and Atlantic Squadron, which assembled at Abrolhos consisted of the two *Invincible* Class Battlecruisers HMS *Invincible* and HMS *Inflexible* and the Light Cruisers HMS *Carnarvon* and HMS *Cornwall*, and the Armoured Cruiser HMS *Kent*, HMS *Macedonia* and HMS *Glasgow*, which was a survivor from the British squadron destroyed by Von Spees' Cruiser Squadron off Coronel just over a month previous. Vice Admiral Sir F.C.D. Sturdee flew his Flag in HMS *Invincible* and the Flag of Rear Admiral A.P. Stoddart flew in HMS *Carnarvon*.

HMS *Cornwall* had joined up with HMS *Carnarvon* at Abrolhos Rocks, Rio de Janeiro, Brazil, on 5 November and was ordered by *Carnarvon* to take on coal. Both ships then departed for Montevideo in Uruguay to join the Armoured Cruiser HMS *Defence* with Rear Admiral Stoddart transferring his Flag to *Defence* on arrival at Montevideo on 10 November. The following day, after coaling, the

British Cruisers began patrols in the River Plate just as HMS *Glasgow* was arriving. While news arrived of the dispatch of two Battlecruisers from home waters and HMS *Kent* from Sierra Leone, the pre-Dreadnought Battleship HMS *Canopus*, which was heading north to join the British squadron at Montevideo, was ordered back to the Falkland Islands to act as guard ship in case the German Cruiser Squadron attacked the Falklands before sufficient British heavy ships were in place. On 11 November, the Armed Merchant Cruiser HMS *Orama* (this ship was commissioned into the Royal Navy on 3 September 1914, having previously served as a passenger ship with the Orient Line) sank the German store ship S.S. *Navarra* off Montevideo after it was set alight when it became clear they could not evade the British ship.

The British Squadron departed Montevideo under command of Admiralty Stoddart on 12 November, bound for Abrolhos Rock, arriving on the 16th. The two Battlecruisers, *Invincible* and *Inflexible*, arrived on 26 November and although they carried orders for HMS *Defence* to sail for St Helena, their presence greatly increased the power of the British Cruiser Squadron, which was to search for Von Spees' Cruisers. With the squadron coaled and stored it departed for Port Stanly in the Falkland Islands on 28 November, with the squadrons Colliers following behind escorted by HMS *Orama*.

The Squadron sailed close to the South American coast with HMS *Bristol* leading, followed by HMS *Kent, Carnarvon, Invincible, Inflexible, Cornwall, Glasgow* and *Macedonia* at 12 mile intervals in staggered formation. The Squadron began arriving at Port William Sound, Port Stanley, on the morning of 7 December, with the first of the Battlecruisers, HMS *Invincible*, arriving at 10.30 am.

The Pre-Dreadnought Battleship HMS *Canopus*, which had taken up station as the Falkland Islands Guard ship, laid a line of improvised mines to protect the new British squadron housed in the specious confines of Port William Sound, although some of the Cruisers went into Port Stanley Harbour. HMS *Canopus* herself had been positioned with fore and aft in such a position that she could effectively use her main armament of four 12-in guns mounted in two turrets – one forward and one aft – by firing overland out to seaward using spotters which had been positioned on shore. She had also landed her Howitzer, which was positioned with other resources such as Maxim Machine Guns to enable the crew and the small Falklands Islands Volunteer Defense Force to oppose any attempted landing by the Von Spees' squadron, should it have arrived before Admiral Sturdee's Squadron arrived.

With their own Colliers following behind, the British squadron arriving almost immediately began to coal from the three Colliers already in the harbour. However, the lack of Colliers then available meant that only three ships could coal at a time; therefore, HMS *Carnarvon*, HMS *Glasgow* and *HMS Bristol* began to coal almost immediately with the other ships waiting in turn, However, there was a delay with the coaling of HMS *Bristol* as the coal was too hot to be put in her bunkers and she had to wait until it was cool enough. The plan was for the two Battlecruisers to take on coal on the morning of 8 December, after which the Squadron would weigh that evening and sail for Cape Horn, with the intention of rounding the Horn and entering the South Pacific in the hope of intercepting Von Spees Squadron before it could round the Horn and enter the South Atlantic. On the 7th, the Squadron had received information, which it was accepted was merely gossip, that the German Squadron had been sighted heading east, bound for the Atlantic.

During the early morning of Sunday 8 December, the British ships continued their preparations to sail that evening to commence the search for the German Cruiser Squadron. The Flagship, *Invincible,* began coaling form a Collier at 05.30.

The sighting of two Cruisers was reported to *Canopus* by telephone between 07.40 and 07.45 am from the signal station ashore at Sapper Hill, *Canopus* then forwarding the information to Admiral Sturdee aboard *Invincible.*"This was routed via HMS Glasgow, which apparently fired a single shot at 07.56 am to attract the attention of HMS *Invincible*, which was coaling at that time. A four-funnel and two-funnel man-of-war in sight, from Sapper Hill, steering northwards". As fate would have it, the German Squadron had found Sturdee's Squadron at anchor in the Falklands, which the Germans assuming a weak defence had planned to raid before continuing northwards.

When the German ships were first sighted the ships of Sturdee's Squadron were in the following positions: the Light Cruiser HMS *Macedonia* was at anchor, acting as look-out ship, the Armoured Cruiser HMS *Kent* was acting as Guard ship lying at anchor in Port William Sound, the Battlecruisers, HMS *Invincible* and HMS *Inflexible,* were both at anchor in Port William Sound, the Light Cruisers HMS *Glasgow* and HMS *Bristol* were both in Port Stanley Harbour. As soon as the German ships were sighted Sturdee ordered HMS *Kent* to weigh as she was at shorter readiness than the other ships. The order was given for all ships to raise steam for full speed in anticipation of a general chase. There was apparently some opinion within the Squadron that the Cruisers may well be Japanese ships, which had rounded the Cape to join the British Squadron. This certainly was the case among Officers of the Cornwall, who when informed of the Cruiser sighting around 08.00 am, continued their breakfast seeing little urgency under the opinion that the ships were probably Japanese.

The crew of *Canopus* went to general quarters. As the two Cruisers were approaching the area deemed appropriate to bombard the wireless station they became visible from *Canopus's* control-top. At 08.10 *Canopus* trained her turrets on approximate bearings. Not long after, as the two German warships continued on course towards Port Stanley, *Canopus* was informed by the signal station on Sapper Hill that three other Cruisers had been spotted to the southward, coming up some miles behind the first two, passing the report on to Admiral Sturdee aboard *Invincible,* who at 08.15 am, had signaled the Squadron, "Raise steam for full speed, report when ready."

Von Spee's Squadron included two Armoured Cruisers, SMS *Scharnhorst* (top) and SMS *Gneisenau*. At the Falklands battle the Squadron included three Light Cruisers including SMS *Dresden* (above).

The first shots of the Falklands battle were fired by the Pre-Dreadnought Battleship HMS *Canopus* (top). Above: HMS *Inflexible* stands by to pick up survivors.

Damage on the Armoured Cruiser HMS Kent following the Falklands battle.

The support of local civilians was proving invaluable as it emerged that the signal station was actually receiving its information from the wife of a sheep farmer, who had dispatched her maid and a House boy atop a hill where they could observe proceedings and relay the information back to Mrs. Felton, who subsequently would telephone the information to the nearest of the signal stations to her, from where the information was passed down to Port Stanley onward to the Flagship. Mrs. Felton and her help would later play a vital part in the events, which would decide the fate of the German Squadrons Colliers.

At 08.45 am, HMS *Kent* left the other British ships in Harbour and proceeded to the entrance where she took up station. A few minutes later at 08.47 am,

Captain Heathcoat S Grant on HMS *Canopus* reported that the original two German ships were now about 8 miles off, while the smoke from the other ships, which were reported at 08.20, appeared to come from at least two ships, which were now some 20 miles from Port Stanley. A third smoke column was reported from the shore based signal station at 08.50 am, again to the southward. Sturdee then ordered HMS *Macedonia* to weigh anchor and position on the inner side of the other ships and then await further orders. There have been reports, some from eye witnesses, that the *Macedonia* was first out on station, nut official records do not support this.

By 09.00 am, the two nearest German Cruisers had been identified, as the Armoured Cruiser SMS *Gneisenau* and the Light Cruiser SMS *Nurnberg*. The Captain of *Canopus* sought permission to open fire on the two initial Cruisers after receiving bearing and elevation information from the shore based observation post. The Flagship ordered *Canopus* to open fire once the Germans ships came into range.

When in the vicinity of Wolf Rocks, the two lead German Cruisers appeared to stop and change course to the North-Eastward. By 09.15 am, the range from the Wireless station to the German cruisers was down to about 11-12,000 yards and it appeared that the German ships were training their guns in the direction of the Wireless Station. On their present course, it appeared to the observers that the German ships would not be at a closer range to HMS *Canopus* than they now were. Although at best the German cruisers were still at extreme range of the *Canopus's* guns, if not out of range, *Canopus* opened fire with both 12-in guns from her forward turret at 09.20 am, in order to throw the German Cruisers off their assumed attack on the wireless station. *Canopus* was hidden from the view of the German ships by a narrow raised strip of land, which she fired over to engage the unwary Germans. *Canopus* fired a total of five, 12-in shells, although, the range was outside the accepted maximum range of the guns at maximum elevation and the shots fell short. The second salvo from the *Canopus* fell some 100 yards short of the *Gneisenau*. The last salvo was fired from extreme elevation of the guns, but still fell short as the German ships were steaming away at high speed increasing the range between themselves and the stationary *Canopus*. Over the years there have been a number of claims that *Canopus* only fired two 12-in practice shells, which were already loaded. This, however, is a fallacy, another in the long succession of fictitious shreds of information that somehow intertwines with factual events. All five shells fired by *Canopus* were live shells. Information garnered from survivors indicated that one of the 12-in shells probably ricocheted of the water and hit the *Gneisenau* at the base of her after funnel, although it is unclear whether it exploded or not. This is probably the source of the false practice shell reports. Survivor statements also indicated that a fragment from a shell exploding in the water may have struck the *Nurnberg*. The part of the *Canopus* is often played-down as a minor part in a modern sea battle played by an obsolete pre-dreadnought battleship. The minor hits achieved by the *Canopus's* guns at extreme range using a rudimentary improvised fire-control system on an obsolete platform were a major achievement. Her role was to act as a fixed harbour defence fort and protect Stanley Harbour from a seaward attack and in this she accomplished her mission to the letter. On the open sea she could be easily outmaneuvered by the German Cruisers, and in all probability torpedoed, but in her grounded defensive position she was unsinkable and her 12-in guns commanded the approaches to Stanley, capable of overpowering anything other than modern Dreadnought battleships.

At this time it appears that the German's were unaware that any British warships were at or near Port Stanley and would have been shocked when HMS *Canopus* suddenly opened fire at a range of 11-12,000 yards. Almost immediately, the two German ships turned away from their original course and hoisted their colours. As these first shots of what became known as the 'Battle of the Falkland Islands' were being fired, the German ships had come into view from the Upper Bridge of the Flagship HMS *Invincible*, which was still lying at anchor behind the low land lying south of Port William at a range of 17,000 yards from the now retiring German ships. The German ships would have by now observed HMS *Kent*, but it was assumed that the Battlecruisers had not been spotted, as a few minutes after turning away, they altered course to port in what appears to have been an attempt to close with and engage HMS *Kent*. However, almost immediately, they again turned away and increased speed, leaving the British to assume they had now spotted the tripod mast that unmistakably characterized the *Invincible* Class Battlecruisers. It was later discovered from German crew members that the Tripod Masts of the Battlecruisers had indeed been spotted, but it remains unclear if this was before or after they had altered course to port towards HMS *Kent*.

It has never been proved conclusively that the Germans intended to land a party ashore or whether they simply planned a bombardment of shore facilities. However, crew from HMS *Canopus* based ashore at the signal station claimed to have observed crew fallen in on the deck of the *Gneisenau* in attire and equipped for a landing. After *Canopus's* initial two shot salvo, the German crew could be seen hurrying to their respective action stations.

At 09.40 am, HMS *Glasgow* weighed with orders to join up with HMS *Kent* and shadow the enemy Cruisers. The *Glasgow* was followed at 09.45 am, by the Battlecruisers, and remainder of the Squadron, excluding HMS *Bristol*. HMS *Carnarvon* was leading, followed by HMS *Inflexible* and then HMS *Invincible* (Flag) and HMS *Cornwall*. Such was the haste to commence the chase of the German Cruisers; *Inflexible* rammed a sailing Pinnacle from HMS *Cornwall*, which had been carrying stores. As the Squadron proceeded past Cape Pembroke Light, the five German warships could be clearly seen to the South-East in the early morning brightness. Maximum visibility was possible because of a clear blue sky and almost flat calm sea, with only a North-Westerly light breeze. These fine conditions would have been a curse to Von Spee, who would have wished for rough, murky overcast weather with plenty of rain-squalls to enable him to evade the British ships. Instead the prevailing conditions, which were ideal for a long-range engagement, must have filled the crews of the German ship with despair

With his ships safely out of their anchorage Admiral Sturdee signaled his ships to commence a general chase at 10.20 am and the last of the ships, HMS *Cornwall* cleared the harbour entrance by 10.30 am, by which time the German ships could be seen on the horizon some 12-13 miles distant, steaming hard to the South-East in an attempt to escape, which Von Spee most probably knew was doomed to inevitable failure. This was not the small area of the North Sea, but the open South Atlantic with its vast areas; time was on the side of the British as they steamed to slowly reduce the gap between them and the fleeing German Cruisers. The *Invincible* was flying the signal "General Chase" and she and *Inflexible* soon overtook HMS *Carnarvon*, and then passed HMS *Kent* as the ships worked up to their maximum speed. *Invincible* and *Inflexible* augmented their coal burners with oil to work up their speed faster, with the result that both were belching out huge volumes of thick acrid black smoke. As the Light Cruiser HMS *Glasgow* was capable of keeping up with the Battlecruisers, steaming at some 25 knots, she was ordered to take up station 2 miles from the Flagship *Invincible*, with *Inflexible* forming on *Invincible's* starboard quarter. HMS *Kent*, *Carnarvon* and *Cornwall* to the rear were steaming at around 22 knots. At 11.15 am, the Battlecruisers and the *Glasgow* reduced speed to 20 knots in order to allow the slower British Cruisers to catch up and take up station, this speed being maintained for around an hour. The *Glasgow* was now taking station around 3 miles ahead of the Flagship. The German Cruisers remained in sight with their funnels and bridges clearly visible above the horizon.

By 12.20 am, the German Cruisers were still well ahead and Sturdee decided to prepare to attack with *Invincible, Inflexible* and *Glasgow*, which had been ordered to close with the Battlecruisers, as the other British Cruisers remained to the rear. At this time, the German Cruisers were proceeding in two separate columns, with the Armoured Cruiser *Gneisenau* and the Light Cruiser *Nurnberg* forming the left column and the Armoured Cruiser Scharnhorst, with the Light Cruisers *Dresden* and *Leipzig* forming the right column. *Leipzig* was now trailing well behind its column with the Germans positioned on the Starboard bow of the British Battlecruisers, which increased speed to around 25 knots, and then pushed out to almost 27 knots to close the range, and at 12.47 pm Sturdee made the signal "Open fire and engage the enemy."

Inflexible was the first to open fire at 12.55 pm, engaging the right-hand German ship (this was the Light Cruiser SMS *Leipzig*) with her forward 12-in gun turret. Within a few minutes *Invincible* opened fire, engaging the same Light Cruiser as *Inflexible*. Fire had commenced at a range of 16,500 yards down to 15,000 yards (between 8 and 9 sea miles). The splashes of the 840-lb 12-in shells fired by Invincible and *Inflexible* rose to a height reported as around 150-feet in the air and at the extreme range almost blotted the targets from view from the observation positions aboard the Battlecruisers. A 12-in shell fell close alongside the *Leipzig* at 1.20 pm and a short time later this ship, in company with the Light Cruiser's SMS *Nurnberg* and *Dresden*, turned away from the German formation heading to the South-West leaving the two German Armoured Cruisers, *Scharnhorst* and *Gneisenau*. This was in accordance with Von Spees' order "The Armoured Cruisers will engage the enemy as long as possible; the light cruisers are to use every endeavour to escape." Prior to the German Light Cruisers breaking from the Armoured Cruisers, the British Battlecruisers claimed a single hit on SMS *Nurnberg*, although it is unclear if this was the case.

The German Light Cruisers were now pursued by HMS *Glasgow, Kent* and *Cornwall*, following orders received from Sturdee. From this point on the Battle would split into several separate actions, not counting the initial engagement of the German ships by HMS *Canopus* that morning.

Invincible and *Inflexible* now turned their attention to the German Armoured Cruisers, which were subjected to a withering fire. At 1.25 pm the German Armoured Cruisers turned some 7 points to port, with *Scharnhorst* in the lead, forming into line ahead to position them to engage the British Battlecruisers; opening fire on the British ships at 1.30 pm. A short time after this, *Invincible* and *Inflexible* reduced speed slightly to 24 knots, after which the two Battlecruisers turned together to bring them into line ahead, with *Invincible* taking the lead. By the time of the final turn the range was down to about 13,500 yards, but again started to increase, reaching about 16,450 yards by 2.00 pm as Vice Admiral Sturdee rightly opted to keep the engagement at maximum range to reduce the effectiveness of the German fire. This round of maneuvering by both opposing Squadrons now brought them onto roughly parallel courses. *Inflexible* had stopped firing for a short period, but now she re-commenced, concentrating on the *Scharnhorst* from a range of some 14,500-yards. Frequently, the British 12-in salvoes fell with a spread of some 200-yards.

The aim for Sturdee was to try and avoid the range between him and his quarry from dropping below 13,500-yards, thereby, reducing the effectiveness of the German guns. Around 1.40 pm, the *Scharnhorst* overhauled the *Gneisenau* and took up the van position resulting on *Invincible* and *Inflexible* swapping targets, with the Flagship now engaging *Scharnhorst* and *Inflexible* engaging the *Gneisenau*. Around this time, both of the German Armoured Cruisers concentrated their combined fire at *Inflexible*, although no results were achieved. Switching their firing back to *Invincible*, the Germans were rewarded with their first hit on the Flagship, which was achieved at around 1.45 pm.

By 2.00 pm, the range had increased to around 16,450-yards, and this, combined with smoke, began to make spotting for the guns more difficult. Unable to close to a range where his guns would be most effective, Von Spee must have decided to again try and escape the British Battlecruisers. At 2.10 pm the German Armoured Cruisers made a turn away about 10 points to starboard to again try and run, to which the British Battlecruisers began to pursue them. By this point in the action it is considered that the *Scharnhorst* had suffered at least three hits based on information from some of the crew, with around 50 casualties. There is no reliable estimate of how many if any hits the *Gneisenau* had sustained.

The increase in range and the resulting chase saw fire being checked for a considerable period of time, until by 2.45 pm the range decreased enough for the Battlecruisers to open fire again from a range of 15,000-yards. Under fire from the British ships, the Germans again turned into line ahead to allow them to bring their guns to bear on the British at 2.53 pm, opening fire with their 8.2-in main armament at 2.55 pm. During this ten minute or so period, the range between the two sides markedly decreased and at one stage was under 12,000-yards. During this exchange of fire the *Scharnhorst* was hit, causing a fire to break out, although this did not look too serious from the position of the British ships. Firing on both sides was furious. "It was like hell let lose," remarked a Petty Officer aboard *Invincible* as British shells fell around and amongst the German ships. The Germans too were inflicting some damage as the *Invincible* sustained several hits. The German gunnery, it was remarked, now seemed less accurate than before, and many shells were landing between the two British Battlecruisers.

Inflexible engaged the *Gneisenau*, which suffered several hits causing considerable damage to the German ship. The *Scharnhorst* was hit a number of times, with one 12-in shell destroying her third funnel, which from the view of the British ships appeared to be "shot away," and fire was seen to start forward around 3.30 pm. Her firing began to slow and some guns were noted to have stopped firing altogether.

With the *Carnarvon* moving up in the rear of the British Battlecruisers, Vice Admiral Sturdee executed a sudden hard maneuver around 3.18 pm. The helm of *Invincible* was put over to starboard and the ship more or less completely turned around so that she crossed her own track. She was now steering a course approximately to the South West. This sudden maneuver had the desired effect of completely throwing the German gunners range out giving the *Invincible* a respite from the many hits she had received up to that point. *Inflexible* had followed *Invincible's* turn with the effect that she was now in the van, with *Invincible* behind; with both ships port beams facing the German ships. Around this time, the *Carnarvon* had been ordered to close with the Battlecruisers using the range lost between them during the Battlecruisers maneuvering to allow her to do this. As her guns were not effective beyond 12,000-yards range, *Carnarvon* had thus far not fired on the enemy ships and the crew was doubtless anxious to participate in the battle against the German Armoured Cruisers, which were again, under heavy fire from the two British Battlecruisers.

At 3.30 pm, *Scharnhorst* turned about 10 points to starboard in what was perceived as an attempt to bring her starboard guns into a firing position. She continued to be hit repeatedly resulting in several fires, some of which were claimed to be visible from the British ships through holes shot in her sides. Her No.3 funnel had been blown away by shell fire as she was pounded by the combined fire of *Invincible* and *Inflexible*. Not long after 3.30 pm, *Inflexible* switched her attention to the *Gneisenau*. By this time the *Scharnhorst* was in a pitiful state, looking like a floating wreck, so severe had the pounding been from the British 12-in shells. However, she was afloat, under steam, and still in the fight. Of the *Scharnhorst,* Admiral Sturdee commented, "At times a shell would cause a large hole to appear in her side, through which could be seen a dull red glow of flame." Despite her severe state of damage, *Scharnhorst* continued to fire her guns in salvoes, a clear sign that she was still under effective command and control, with her starboard guns now firing frequently since they were able to be brought to bear. The range was 14,000-yards, and such was the severe plight of the *Scharnhorst* that at 3.56 pm, Sturdee ordered his ships to close the range to finish her off. This now allowed HMS *Carnarvon* to come into effective range for her guns, and she joined the onslaught against the *Scharnhorst*.

The pounding from the British ships became too much and by 4.00 pm *Scharnhorst* was seen to have all three funnels destroyed and both masts brought down, then at 4.04 pm she suddenly took on a heavy list to port. Although she remained under power and moving the list continued to increase, until by 4.10 pm she was lying on her port-beam with the engines still producing power and turning her screws. She remained on her side for some seven minutes before suddenly sinking beneath the waves at 4.17 pm, having never struck her colours, which remained flying as she went down. A few minutes before she sank the British ships ceased fire on her and switched their attention to the *Gneisenau*.

During this time the British Flagship turned two full circles in a more or less figure of eight pattern and it looked as though the *Gneisenau* was going to attempt to rescue survivors from the *Scharnhorst*. However, unless she struck her colours, this would have invited sure and speedy destruction at the hands of the British Battlecruisers. The *Gneisenau* decided to continue the completely mismatched fight in accordance with Von Spees original order of fighting for as long as they could to aid the attempted escape of the German Light Cruisers. As *Invincible* had now turned onto a course in the general direction of the *Scharnhorst*, the crew of the *Gneisenau* may have been under the impression that she was moving in to pick up survivors from the *Scharnhorst* and did not engage her, instead opening fire on the *Inflexible*. However, the cruelness of war inevitably reared its head as the British still had the *Gneisenau* to deal with, which it was decided took precedence over the rescue of enemy sailors. HMS *Carnarvon* passed through the area where the *Scharnhorst* had been seen to sink some 15 minutes after she sank, but could find no trace of survivors or of wreckage. The crew had perished to a man in their gallant fight against overwhelming odds.

With the German Flagship gone, the remaining Armoured Cruiser, *Gneisenau*, remained defiant in her fight against the two British Battlecruisers, both of which could now turn their attention to the single German ship, which was determined to go down fighting to the end. Against such odds, *Gneisenau* had no realistic chance, but continued the fight suffering further damage and casualties. The fine morning and early afternoon weather now began to change as drizzle reduced the range at, which the enemy could be easily observed.

After a pause in firing, *Invincible* had re-commenced firing on *Gneisenau* at 4.15 pm, which herself was engaging the *Inflexible*, but now turned her attention to *Invincible*. By 4.25 pm, *Gneisenaus'* salvoes were straddling the *Invincible*, taking advantage of the reduction in range which had now dropped to around 10,000-yards, before the British again began to open the range. The *Gneisenau* was repeatedly hit, causing immense carnage on-board. However, the firing was still very much two way traffic and between 4.25 and 4.40 pm *Invincible* sustained three hits. The *Gneisenaus'* colours had been brought down by British shell fire several times and then re-hoisted by her crew. They were again brought down by shell fire and she stopped firing at 4.47 pm. The feeling aboard the British Flagship was that she had now struck her colours as she was in an awful state of twisted metals, beams, plates and a scene of pure carnage, although from the British ships she looked remarkably undamaged in comparison to the *Scharnhorst's* state before she sank. On-board *Gneisenau* it must have seemed like Dante's Hell, as the concentrated fire of two Battlecruisers rained down.

As the British Battlecruisers maneuvered so as not to allow the range to increase, *Gneisenau* quite suddenly and unexpectedly fired a single shot. She had not given up after all; it was simply that she had actually run out of colours, which was why no more were hoisted. For the Germans, this had always been a fight to the finish, for which there could only be one outcome. This was a fact to which they must had resigned themselves early in the action, which speaks volumes for the gallantry of the commanders and ordinary seamen alike.

The end could not now be far-off, and at 5.08 pm *Gneisenaus'* forward funnel was hit; falling over and coming to rest against her second funnel. By this time her fire had slowed considerably as she reeled under the continuous barrage from the British Battlecruisers and HMS *Carnarvon*. She was, however, still capable of hitting back and at 5.15 pm one of her shells struck HMS *Invincible*. However, by now she was obviously in trouble having suffered a number of hits, including one between her third and fourth funnels. The situation on deck must have been well nigh intolerable, yet it was tolerated as her upper works were wrecked by shell after shell and her decks could be seen to be ripped up even from the range at which the British observed her. At 5.30 pm she turned towards *Invincible* and appeared to have stopped, having taken on a heavy list to starboard with several fires burning and smoke and steam from fractured pipes rising into the air. Vice Admiral Sturdee reported that he then issued the signal "Cease fire", but that *Gneisenau* began firing on the British ships again before the signal could be hoisted. This firing from *Gneisenau* was from a single gun, which continued to fire intermittently. The British ships closed in on *Gneisenau* at 5.40 pm, continuing to fire on the German ship, which replied with a single shot at around 5.45 pm; her last shot of the battle. After this her guns remained silent. According to Sturdee's report, around this time the German flag, which had been flying from the "fore truck", came down, although the flag at the "peak" remained in position. Sturdee gave the signal "Cease fire," at 5.50 pm. *Gneisenaus'* fate had been sealed, and at 6.00 pm she suddenly heeled over, lying on her side.

The crew, like that of the *Scharnhorst* had gallantly fought to the bitter end, bringing admiration from their enemy for their gallant, but futile struggle against the odds. Surviving crew could be seen climbing onto the ships upper side, as she settled with the British ships about 4,000-yards off at this time. After a minute or two on her side, she slowly slide beneath the waves with steam gushing from her interior as the survivors went into the water hoping to be rescued. The official time of her foundering was 6.02 pm, in position Latitude 52 degrees 42' S., Longitude 56 degree 20' W.

The British ships now moved in to rescue the survivors, but the weather had deteriorated and the sea was getting up quite a bit. An estimated 200 men had been seen on her decks before she had heeled over onto her side, but many of these perished in the water as she capsized. British ships lowered boats to try and rescue as many men in the water as possible. *Invincible* took aboard 108 men, 14 of whom were unfortunately dead by the time they were brought on board. Others were rescued, although many of them in the water either drowned or died of exposure in the extremely cold temperatures of the South Atlantic.

Prisoner reports indicated that the carnage on *Gneisenau* had been terrible. By the time she had run out of ammunition some 600 men had apparently been killed, with many wounded. Reports from *Gneisenau* survivors also stated that the splash from near-misses from British 12-in shells actually extinguished some fires that had been started as a result of earlier hits. Splashes from near misses are also claimed to have so flooded the gun turrets of the *Gneisenau* that the main armament gunners had to work knee deep in water during the battle. The Survivor accounts also showed that the British 12-in lyddite bursting shell was a devastating weapon, with reports that they caused carnage among the German crews. Survivor reports indicated that a 12-in lyddite shell severed one of *Gneisenaus'* gun turrets from its "trunk" before it fell overboard.

According to crew reports *Invincible* was hit over 20 times, although some of these would have been merely fragments from shells bursting in the water. What is clear is that she suffered 18 direct hits and at least 4 indirect hits. An 8.2-in shell, which came in at an estimated angle of 50 degrees hit one of *Invincible's* 4-in secondary battery guns positioned just abaft the fore bridge, cutting the muzzle clean off, before it continued on to penetrate the deck, on through a ventilation vent and through the next deck before coming to rest in the

Admirals store room without bursting. Another shell hit her side leaving a huge hole before penetrating on to wreck the wardroom. She was hit by two shells on the after conning tower stalk. It was reported that both shells burst and caused damage, but caused no casualties within the after conning tower. However, it is reasonably certain that only one exploded. The tower was filled with smoke fumes, which although affecting the inhabitants caused no long lasting effects. The inhabitants of the tower also noted that when the shell burst there was significant vibration, but the instruments were not affected. A shell had penetrated through part of the tripod mast close to the conning tower. Another shell hit below the waterline causing a hole some 7-ft in by 4-ft in diameter, which caused flooding of one of her coal bunkers. *Invincible* also suffered extensive damage to the sick bay.

Inflexible apparently sustained only direct hits during the battle; her main derrick was sliced in two removing her ability to use her steam boats. Two of the direct hits on Invincible were below the waterline on the port side, one of which resulted in a bunker flooding causing a small list, although her seaworthiness was not seriously affected. *Invincible* suffered no casualties, while *Inflexible* suffered one killed and three wounded; none serious.

This photograph purports to show the Crew of the SMS *Nurnberg* surrendering to the British warships. Of course in reality the battle was over when the ship went down and the crews are here being picked rescued by their former assailants.

While the Battlecruisers had been engaged with the German Armoured Cruisers, the British Light Cruisers and the Armoured Cruiser HMS *Kent* had embarked upon a pursuit of the three German Light Cruisers. *Carnarvon* had stayed with the Battlecruisers as she did not possess the necessary speed to catch any of the three German Light Cruisers.

When they detached from Spees' Armoured Cruisers, the three German Light Cruisers were in the following formation: *Leipzig* was in the centre, but further back than the others, with *Nurnberg* positioned around one mile on her port bow, but ahead, with *Dresden* about five miles or so on her starboard bow being much further ahead. Both the *Dresden* and *Nurnberg* were straying slightly out from *Leipzig* as all three ships were effectively going their separate ways in their desperate attempt to escape the more powerful British Cruisers.

As the British Cruisers set out after their quarry, HMS *Cornwall* and *Kent* were trailing the *Leipzig* by about 11 miles as they raced to try and close the range with the German ships. While the *Cornwall* and *Kent* were effectively side by side in close proximity, *Glasgow* was positioned about four miles on their starboard bow, and with her higher speed was in a much better position to run down any of the three German ships, with *Leipzig* being the obvious target as it was the closest. *Glasgow* was the fastest ship in any of the two opposing forces, and this high speed was soon to tell as she overtook the *Kent* and *Cornwall*, closing to around 12,000 yards by 3.00 pm when she opened fire with her 6-in main battery on SMS *Leipzig* (other reports state the range as 10,000 yards when the Glasgow opened fire).

Leipzig, effectively caught and unable to outrun the *Glasgow*, was also outgunned having a main battery of 4.2-in guns, while the *Glasgow* had a much heavier punch with her 6-in armament main armament. The German Cruiser then opened fire on Glasgow, also turning to close the range a bit. This enabled *Cornwall* to close the range between her and the engagement between *Glasgow* and *Leipzig* faster than would have been the case otherwise. There were another two, short duration, long-range engagements between *Glasgow* and *Leipzig*, by which time *Cornwall* was within range.

During the engagement between *Glasgow* and *Leipzig*, HMS *Cornwall* and *Kent* had been closing on the *Glasgow* and at 3.36, *Cornwall* instructed *Kent* to break off and pursue SMS *Nurnberg*, while she continued to close with the *Glasgow* and engage the *Leipzig*, opening fire at 4.17 pm, her shots falling short. By this time, the *Glasgow* had closed to a range of 9,000 yards from *Leipzig*, with the German ship starting to get Glasgow's range. *Glasgow* now turned a "half circle" in order to bring her other battery into action, opening fire with effective results on the *Leipzig*, which was now on the *Glasgow's*' port side. The *Glasgow* then crossed the *Cornwall's* stern in order to come up on the *Leipzig's* other quarter. While *Leipzig* was pre-occupied with engaging the *Cornwall*, the *Glasgow* opened fire, hitting and straddling her with several salvos.

Eventually *Leipzig's* firing slackened as she suffered from her beating at the hands of *Glasgow* and *Cornwall* as well as a lack of ammunition for her guns. *Leipzig*, which was now heavily on fire, ceased firing at 7.30 pm. The ship looked finished, but as her colours still appeared to be flying the British ships continued a storm of 6-in gunfire into her before firing ceased. The *Glasgow*, it is then claimed, tried to communicate with Leipzig to ask if she wanted to surrender, but apparently received no reply, resulting in the *Glasgow* opening fire on her again. At this, *Glasgow* and *Cornwall* closed to a range of around 5,000 yards and began firing lyddite, which caused horrendous carnage among the *Leipzig's* crew. *Leipzig* was now almost completely engulfed in fire and smoke and was obviously in a state of sinking, therefore, *Glasgow* again ceased firing. Boats were lowered and some of *Leipzig's* crew was rescued, with the ship sinking around 9.00 pm. The survivors revealed that *Leipzig* had fired her last round before 7.30 pm and had then tried to surrender to save life, but could not get the British to understand their signals. *Cornwall* reported that just after 8.00 pm signals of distress were observed on *Leipzig* and that she foundered at 9.23 just as darkness was closing in.

By the time the British ships stopped firing for the last time, some 300 of *Leipzig's* crew had been killed with only around 320 still alive, some 12 of which drowned as the ship went down. Many of the crew had been killed after *Leipzig* had run out of ammunition and tried to surrender. The crew was assembling on the forecastle in anticipation of being taken off the stricken ship when the *Glasgow* opened fire again killing some 60 men assembled on the forecastle. *Glasgow's* casualties were one killed, four badly wounded and several slightly wounded with only very slight damage.

A 4.1-in shell from the *Leipzig* hit the *Cornwall*, which passed through a 3/eighths of an in thick depression rail of the after 6-in turret, was deflected from its original path, going through the deck approximately at a bulkhead separating two cabins before continuing through the next deck and bursting against the side of the ship, resulting in a fairly large hole. Another 4.1-in shell, which exploded below the waterline, resulted in flooding of two bunkers. From inside the ship there was a 5-in indentation located around five to six feet below *Cornwall's* waterline, in a location below the armour belt. As there was no sign of any external damage, even to the paintwork it was assumed that the shell did not hit, but was a near miss.

According to a report from HMS *Cornwall*, both *Cornwall* and *Kent* opened fire on the *Leipzig* at 4.15 pm, both ships firing almost simultaneously at a range of around 11,000 yards. It was a few minutes after this, noted as 4.17 pm that *Kent* detached and set off after the *Nurnberg*.

While the *Cornwall* and *Glasgow* were engaging the *Leipzig*, HMS *Kent* was in pursuit of the *Nurnberg* and had closed to within effective firing range by 5.00 pm. HMS *Kent* opened fire from long-range, but continued to close the range, taking advantage of a reduction in speed by the *Nurnberg*. Once range was down to about 5,000 yards the *Kent* and *Nurnberg* exchanged a number of very rapid salvoes, with both ships being hit a number of times. The *Kent* continued to close the range, overpowering *Nurnberg* with her heavier guns, until by around 6.35 pm *Nurnberg* was on fire with no guns firing. "Cease fire" was ordered on the *Kent*, which then closed to a range of 3,300 yards, at which it was determined that *Nurnberg's* colours were still flying, therefore, HMS Kent re-commenced firing for some five minutes before ceasing as *Nurnberg's* colours appeared to have been struck. *Nurnberg* sank sometime between 7.10 and 7.27 pm (accounts differ between official documents and eye witness accounts) with only twelve of her crew being rescued from the water, five of which were either dead or died later. Casualties on *HMS Kent* consisted of four killed and twelve wounded (various documents state differing numbers such as eight killed and 12 wounded), most of which appeared to have been the result of one shell from the *Nurnberg*.

Although she suffered relatively light casualties, HMS *Kent* suffered much damage, with her upper works pockmarked with holes and her fore-top mast being brought down by a shell, which resulted in her wireless being put out of action. However, her waterline remained intact, although there was some damage, and her engines had not been damaged.

During the various engagements it was noted that the German guns were able to achieve long ranges; this due to their mountings, which were able to achieve elevations in the order of thirty degree's. It was also noted that the spread of their salvoes was much less than those of the British guns indicating superior guns and or gun mountings and or superior ballistic qualities of their shells. The Germans were also able to achieve a very high speed of rapid fire.

The ammunition expenditure for the Battlecruisers was noted as 661 x 12-in shells fired from Inflexible, with Invincible firing 513 x 12-in shells.

No Torpedoes were fired by any side during the battles and German survivor reports claimed that only the *Scharnhorst* and *Gneisenau* carried any mines.

With the British squadron in hot pursuit of the German Cruisers, the Captain of *Canopus* decided to raise the ship off the mud and un-ground her on the evening tide in case she were needed at sea. However, with the news that all but one of the German ships had been caught and sunk this plan was dropped with *Canopus* remaining grounded.

Although she would have been unable to put to sea before the high tide of 9.00 pm, which would be the only way to un-ground her, HMS *Canopus's* role in the destruction of the German ships was not over yet. Being in telephone communications with the land based posts, *Canopus* was acting as a communications hub reporting between land based observation positions and the British warships. At 10.50 am the Falkland Islands Governor telephoned,

Canopus reporting that he had received a report from an observation post of three merchant ships off Port Pleasant, Fitzroy, to the south west of Port Stanley Harbour. *Canopus* then signaled HMS *Macedonia* "Three enemy merchant transports off Port Pleasant, Fitzroy. Ask permission from Admiral to chase them." After receiving permission *Macedonia* informed *Canopus* that she was steaming towards the German ships at 11.25 am, with HMS *Bristol*, which had been forced to remain behind when the British Squadron went off after the German Cruisers, following soon after. *Canopus* was by now in direct telephone communication with Fitzroy, receiving information on the German Merchant ships course, which she then passed on to the *Macedonia* and *Bristol*, which were in hot pursuit. The information from Fitzroy was actually being passed on to *Canopus* by two local women located at Port Darwin, with one of the women observing the enemy ships and the other staying with the telephone and passing the information to the *Canopus*.

At 11.27 am HMS *Bristol* signaled that three German ships had appeared off Port Pleasant. These were the German Cruiser Squadrons Collier's and supply ships, although in the event there were only two vessels and not three as was initially reported. Sturdee placed HMS *Macedonia* under the *Bristol's* orders and ordered the two British Cruisers to destroy the German merchant ships, which were the steamships *Baden* and *Santa Isabel*. The crews of these ships were taken off before they were sunk by the British ships.

Following the various engagements, the *Bristol* and *Macedonia* were the first of the British squadron to return to Stanley on 9 December, followed by *Glasgow* and *Cornwall*. As *Kent* had had her wireless knocked out and was therefore, not able communicate with the remaining ships or with port, there was some worry that she had been sunk, until news of her arrived that her wireless had been destroyed, although she had, it was reported suffered a hit on one of her casemates and was damaged on the waterline. Once back at Staley a work party from the *Canopus* was sent aboard the *Kent* to effect temporary repairs to the holed waterline.

On 13 December, HMS *Inflexible, Glasgow* and *Bristol* departed Stanley to commence a search for the *Dresden*, which had escaped during the battle of a few days previous. At this time the best information available led the British to think she may have been in the vicinity of Punta Arenas, southern Chile.

On the afternoon of 16 December, HMS *Invincible* departed Port Stanley, with Armed Merchant Cruiser HMS *Otranto,* under Captain H McL. Edwards, arriving the same day. The 16th also saw *Canopus* being un-grounded from her mud-bed and moored at Stanley, taking on coal on the 17th before departing for Abrolhos on the 18th. During the journey to Abrolhos *Canopus* remained in wireless contact with *Invincible*, which was steaming ahead of her, but further inshore. *Canopus* eventually arrived at Abrolhos Rocks on 26 December 1914, where she again joined HMS *Invincible*, which had arrived there a short time before, and was taking on coal from two colliers. *Invincible* departed Abrolhos Rocks on 27 December, bound for Gibraltar. *Inflexible*, having left the search for *Dresden* to the *Glasgow* and other Cruisers arrived at Abrolhos Rocks on 31 December to take on coal before departing bound for Gibraltar. Much to the consternation of the *Canopus*, *Inflexible* used her wireless to announce her pending arrival while she was still some way off. Due to the constant reports of possible German ships in the area, *Canopus* wanted the presence of heavy British warships at Abrolhos to be as inconspicuous as possible.

Probably for the first and last time, Abrolhos Rocks played host to a third Battlecruiser in just over two weeks when the *Indefatigable Class* Battlecruiser *HMAS Australia* arrived to coal on 11-12 January 1915, before continuing her journey to the United Kingdom. The Arrogant Class Protected Cruiser HMS *Vindictive* arrived on 14 January to relive the *Canopus*, which then left bound for St Vincent. The Armed Merchant Cruiser HMS *Celtic*, delivered ammunition for *Invincible* and *Inflexible* at St Vincent, before she went on to Abrolhos Rock.

British Squadron

Battlecruisers - HMS *Invincible* and HMS *Inflexible*

Pre-Dreadnought Battleship - HMS *Canopus*

Armoured Cruisers - HMS *Kent* (*Monmouth* Class) and HMS *Carnarvon* (*Devonshire* Class)

Light Cruisers - HMS *Glasgow*, HMS *Bristol* and HMS *Cornwall*

Auxiliary Cruiser - HMS *Macedonia*

German Squadron

Armoured Cruisers - SMS *Gneisenau* and SMS *Scharnhorst*

Light Cruisers - SMS *Leipzig*, SMS *Dresden* and SMS *Nurnberg*

6

THE NORTH SEA AND ATLANTIC - 1 JANUARY 1915 TO 30 JUNE 1915

As 1914 was ending more reliable information from "directional wireless stations and of wireless telegraphy", along with breakthroughs in the intelligence gathering system from the department of the Director of Intelligence at the Admiralty, under Rear-Admiral Henry F. Oliver, reduced the previous requirement of having the Grand Fleet at or preparing for sea on an almost constant basis. This was very welcome for the various Squadrons, as it would allow more time in port to conduct maintenance and non-sea training. The new intelligence system and directional wireless stations among other things, it was hoped, would give the Admiralty enough warning to counter any large scale movements into the North Sea by the German High Seas Fleet.

Without the need for the constant patrolling by the Battle Squadrons the Dreadnought elements of the Battle Fleet remained at Scapa Flow until 10 January. The Battlecruisers were more active in the first few weeks of 1915. HMS *Princess Royal* returned to the UK on 1 January, following her period of service on the North American Station. From the 3rd of January, the 1st Battle Cruiser Squadron, along with the 1st Light Cruiser Squadron, conducted a sweep of the central area of the North Sea, returning to Rosyth on the 5th.

On 15 January 1915, the 2nd Battle Cruiser Squadron was officially reformed again at Rosyth, under the command of Vice-Admiral Sir A. G. W. Moore, K.C.B., who raised his flag in HMS *New Zealand*, following its transfer from HMS *Leviathan* of the 1st Cruiser Squadron. When formed, the strength of the 2nd Battle Cruiser Squadron was given on paper as consisting of HMS *New Zealand* (Flagship), HMS *Indomitable* and HMS *Invincible*, although the latter ship had not yet returned from its spell in the South Atlantic. Only HMS *New Zealand* and *Indomitable* were available, and one of these had problems with her electronic gear.

The 1st and 2nd Battle Cruiser Squadrons, along with the 1st Light Cruiser Squadron, left Rosyth on 17 January to conduct a sweep of the central and southern North Sea; it had been reported that a force of German Destroyers were patrolling between the Horn Reef and the Elms Canal. The British Squadrons also had orders to be in position, Latitude 55 N., Longitude 5.30 E., at daybreak on the 19th, to support the light forces under Commodore Tyrwhitt, which were conducting a reconnaissance sweep of the Heligoland Bight. This sweep proved uneventful, with the only sightings of enemy forces being a Zeppelin airship and a Seaplane on the 18th.

The Zeppelin shadowed the Battlecruisers at a distance of around 20 miles and a single Seaplane approached the force, being engaged by the HMS *Lions* Anti Aircraft "Pom Pom" and a single shrapnel round from one of her forward 13.5-in guns. This was described as whizzing out and exploding in the air like a huge firework. The Seaplane was seen to shudder in the air from the force of the blast, which was about a quarter of a mile away, before she turned away from the British ships. The Battlecruisers then participated in two days of exercises with the Harwich Force, which included 4-in gunnery firing and rangefinder exercises, before returning to Rosyth in company with the 1st Light Cruiser Squadron, arriving during the course of the night of 20/21 January.

Another sweep of the southern North Sea commenced on 23 January when the 1st and 2nd Battle Cruiser Squadrons and the 1st Light Cruiser Squadron departed Rosyth to rendezvous with the light forces of the Harwich Force. HMS *Queen Mary* was absent from the 1st Battle Cruiser Squadron at this time as she was undergoing a refit. The Battle Fleet and supporting units of the Grand Fleet sailed from Scapa and other bases to support this operation. The Flagship, HMS *Iron Duke,* along with the 1st, 2nd and 4th Battle Squadrons, the 1st, 2nd and 6th Cruiser Squadrons, the 2nd Light Cruiser Squadron and the 28 available Destroyers from the 2nd and 4th Flotillas departed during the evening of 23 January, heading into the North Sea for the planned rendezvous with the Harwich Force.

The 3rd Battle Squadron, along with the 3rd Cruiser Squadron operated away from the main Battle Fleet and was ordered to sail to the area of the rendezvous point for the Battlecruisers and the Harwich Force.

The Battle of the Dogger Bank – January 1915

At 7.00 am on 24 January 1914, the Battle Cruiser force commanded by Beatty, consisting of the 1st Battle Cruiser Squadron, HMS *Lion* (Flagship), HMS *Tiger* and HMS *Princess Royal*; and the 2nd Battle Cruiser Squadron, HMS *New Zealand* (Flying the flag of Rear-Admiral Sir Archibald Moore, KCB, CVO) and HMS *Indomitable;* and the 1st Light Cruiser Squadron, HMS *Southampton* (flying the broad pennant of Commodore W. E.Goodenough, MVO), HMS *Nottingham*, HMS *Lowestoft* and HMS *Birmingham*, passed through position 55.13 N 3.12 E, (position of the flagship HMS *Lion*), with the 1st Light Cruiser Squadron positioned some 5 miles on *Lion's* port beam. The three squadrons were steaming a course of S. 12 W., at a speed of 18 knots.

Once through 55.13 N., 3.12 E., Beatty ordered the 1st Light Cruiser Squadron to spread out and position itself for "look out duties" N.E. by N. At 07.10 am, Commodore (T) R Tyrwhitt in HMS *Arethusa*, in company with half a Flotilla of Destroyers was sighted by Beatty. At 07.25 am, Beatty's force observed the flash of gunfire at S.S.E. A short time later Beatty received a report which informed him that the *Arethusa* Class Light Cruiser HMS Aurora was involved in an engagement with German warships. He immediately ordered his force onto a course S.S.E. and increased speed to 22 knots. The Light Cruisers and Destroyer Flotilla were ordered to "chase" S.S.E. and provide reports on movements of enemy vessels. Beatty began receiving reports almost immediately from HMS *Southampton*, *Arethusa* and *Aurora* as to the nature of the enemy force, which was reported as being four Battlecruisers supported by 6 Light Cruisers and an unknown number of Destroyers, originally on a N.W. course, although this had now changed to a S.E. course.

Once visual contact had been made Beatty's Light Cruisers were able to maintain contact and report the various movements of the German force as he ordered his Battlecruisers to work up to full speed and maneuver in an attempt to get into the leeward position, with the secondary aim of getting between the German ships and their base, and possibly force them northward further away from base. At this time, conditions were fine, with visibility reported as extreme and only a light N.E. wind.

At 07.50 am, Beatty sighted the four German Battlecruisers on his (HMS *Lions*) port bow. At this time the enemy vessels were steaming at high speed on an approximately S.E. heading, some 14 miles from Beatty's Battlecruisers. With constant reports on the German ships positions Beatty achieved his position of advantage on the lee quarter of the German Battlecruisers. He therefore ordered his force to alter course and then began the stern chase. The British Battlecruiser's increased speed until the 1st Battle Cruiser Squadron had reached 28.5 knots, while the slower HMS *New Zealand* and *Indomitable* in the 2nd Battle Cruiser Squadron began to lag behind slightly, although this was not as much as has often been reported. The *New Zealand* actually achieved 27 knots and *Indomitable* achieved 26 knots, which were above the design speed of both ships, enabling them to remain not too far astern of the 1st Battle Cruiser Squadron.

At 08.52 am, Beatty closed to under 20,000 yards of the rearmost of the four German Battlecruisers as the British Battlecruisers maneuvered "on a line of bearing" so that their guns would bear. HMS *Lion* was the first to engage, firing a single 13.5-in shell, which fell short of the target, the rearmost of the German ships, which were steaming in single line ahead. The German Light Cruisers were ahead of the German Battlecruisers and their Destroyers were positioned on their starboard beam. HMS *Lion* continued to fire single 13.5-in shells at various intervals to try and get the range, claiming to achieve the first hit on the rearmost German Battlecruiser, SMS *Blucher* (This ship was more accurately classed as a modern Armoured Cruiser, inferior in firepower and speed to the Battlecruisers), at 09.09 am. HMS *Tiger* opened fire on the *Blucher* at 09.20 am as HMS *Lion* shifted her fire to the 3rd ship in the German Battlecruiser line, which was at a range of 18,000 yards. Beatty claimed that *Lion* hit this ship with several salvos. At 09.28 am, the first of the German ships returned fire, targeting HMS *Lion*. By this time HMS *Princess Royal* was within firing range and commenced firing on the *Blucher*. Before long three of the German Battlecruisers were firing at HMS *Lion*, with the closest at a range of 17,500 yards. By 09.35 am, HMS *New Zealand* had come into firing range of the *Blucher*, which was beginning to fall behind the other three German Battlecruisers; therefore, Beatty issued a signal, "Engage the corresponding ships in the enemy's line". As HMS *New Zealand* commenced firing on the *Blucher* HMS *Princess Royal* shifted her fire to the third ship in the German Battlecruiser line, claiming many hits on her.

In the meantime the 1st Light Cruiser Squadron and Destroyer Flotilla had slowly dropped back into a position "broad on our beam to our port quarter"; HMS *Lions*, in order that their smoke did not interfere with the ranging of the British Battlecruisers. However, concerned that the German Destroyers were about to attack Beatty ordered Commodore (T) to position himself ahead. He was, however, unable to achieve this position without steering between the British and German Battlecruisers resulting in smoke obscuring the British Battlecruisers firing. Later HMS *Meteor* leading 'M' Division did manage to pass ahead of the British Battlecruisers due mainly to her high speed.

By 09.45 am, the *Blucher* had sustained many hits and was clearly showing signs of the battering she was taking. Beatty claimed that the leading German Battlecruiser and the No.3 in the line were on fire at this time. HMS *Lion* was targeting the No.1 ship in the German line, *Princess Royal* engaged the No.3 and *New Zealand* engaged the *Blucher*, which was trailing behind the other three German ships in the line. HMS *Tiger*, which should have engaged the No.2 ship in the German line, actually joined HMS *Lion* in engaging the No.1 ship until smoke began to interfere with her aim and she switched fire to the No.3 in the line, which was also being engaged by HMS *Princess Royal*. This left the No.2 ship in the German line unmolested and she concentrated her fire on HMS *Lion*.

Beatty now concluded that the German Battlecruisers had altered course to the northward under the cover of the smoke screen being laid down by their Destroyers, with the aim of increasing their distance from the British Battlecruisers. He definitely concluded that the rearmost German ships had now hauled out of the straight line ahead formation onto the port quarter of the lead German Battlecruiser, with the effect that they had increased their distance from the British Battlecruiser line. In an attempt to counter this Beatty ordered his Battlecruisers into a formation on a line of bearing of N.N.W. and to increase speed to maximum speed to close the range between them and the German Battlecruisers. At this point it appeared to Beatty that the German Destroyers were preparing to launch an attack on HMS *Lion*, however, they were engaged by the *Lions* 4-in secondary battery and the 6-in secondary battery of HMS *Tiger*, with the latter being particularly effective in forcing the German Destroyers to retire. Beatty reported that the 6-in guns of the *Tiger* engaged the Destroyers at long range and put at least two salvoes among the Destroyer formation at a range of 12,000 yards. Beatty then attempted to close the range between his Battlecruisers and the German Battlecruisers by altering course to port, but this was continually countered by the German Torpedo Craft turning more to Starboard, putting Beatty's ships in a position which they would be forced to cross the Torpedo Craft's tracks, a situation which had to be avoided unless absolutely necessary owing to the danger of the Germans laying mines in the path of the British Battlecruisers. Beatty was therefore increasingly reliant on maintaining sufficient speed to try and force the German Battlecruisers northward.

During the course of the engagement the Light Cruisers of the 1st Light Cruiser Squadron had maintained a position on the port quarter of the German Battlecruiser formation. This put them in a good position in which to observe the enemy and to engage any of the ships that fell out of the German line. It also allowed them to provide reports on the fall of shot for Beatty's Battlecruisers. For instance the Light Cruiser HMS *Southampton* reported one of the British Battlecruisers (generally considered to be HMS *Tiger*) was consistently firing over the German ships.

A high level of German fire was directed at HMS *Lion*, particularly from 10.00 am as she was receiving fire from the two leading Battlecruisers in the German line. The British ships then made two slight course alterations of one point inwards, following which HMS *Lion* then conducted a zig-zag pattern in an attempt to throw off the German aim, which had been finding the *Lion*. However, at 10.40 am HMS *Lion* was hit a number of times, suffering much damage resulting in the port engine being stopped by 10.51 am. With all lighting out, she was taking on water, resulting in a heavy list to port. With the damage and loss of power in the port engine *Lion* could no longer maintain her position in the British line

By this time the *Blucher* had sustained significant damage and was lagging well behind the other German Battlecruisers. At 10.48 am she was on fire and had a significant list when she dropped out of the German line to port and steered to the north. It seemed that the *Blucher* was effectively finished and Beatty ordered HMS *Indomitable*, which was in the rear of the British Battlecruiser line, to steer north and engage the crippled *Blucher*.

The threat from German Submarines was brought to the fore when reports of sighting's were received at 10.54 am, and Beatty himself claimed to have personally observed the "wash of a periscope" two points on the *Lion's* starboard bow. He therefore signaled the British Battlecruisers to "turn 8 points to port together", with the signal being taken down at 11.00 am. The new course would take the British Battlecruisers across the track of the German Destroyers, therefore, the British had to make the turn large enough to avoid any mines the German ships might drop when they saw the turn being initiated. Around 11.00 am, *Indomitable* reported that she had observed the track of a torpedo which had been launched at her. This apparently crossed her bows at a distance of 40 yards ahead of her track "after the vicinity of the sinking *Blucher*".

At 11.02 am Beatty hoisted the signal "Course NE", which would cut the German ships off from the *Blucher* if they chose to turn to support her as Beatty later stated he thought they would do. If the *Blucher* was abandoned by the German force then the plan was for the British Battlecruisers to turn back onto a parallel course once they had cleared the track of the German Torpedo craft.

By 11.03 am it was clear that HMS *Lions* condition was serious enough that she could not be repaired at sea and would be unable to continue to provide much in the ongoing battle. Beatty, therefore, ordered her to proceed on a North West course. He semaphored Commodore (T) ordering him to close the *Lion* and provide Destroyers as a Submarine screen.

At 11.05 am Beatty hoisted the signal "Attack the enemy's rear", at the same time taking down the course signal and hoisting another signal "Keep nearer to the enemy". With HMS *Lions* wireless gear out of commission and only signal hallards remaining available, Beatty was not able to inform Admiral Moore of the reasons for his recent maneuvers and it removed his ability to adequately continue to exercise command of the Squadron. He opted to keep the two signals "Attack the enemy's rear" and "Keep nearer the enemy" hoisted until the entire Battlecruiser Squadron had passed and was effectively out of sight.

With the *Lion* effectively out of the battle Beatty ordered the Destroyer HMS *Attack* alongside to take him off at 11.20 am, and he transferred his Flag to HMS *Attack* at 11.35 am. HMS *Attack* then steamed at top speed to join with the British Battlecruiser's which were met at noon while retiring on a course N.N.W. Beatty signaled for the British Battlecruisers to conduct a 16 points turn and resume the pursuit of the three remaining German Battlecruisers, after which he transferred from HMS *Attack* to HMS *Princess Royal*. At 12.20 pm, when Captain Brooke of *Princess Royal* briefed him on what had transpired since *Lion* had fell out of the British Battlecruiser line: *Blucher* had been sunk while the remaining three German Battlecruisers had escaped on an eastward course in damaged condition. He also reported that the ships rescuing the crew of the *Blucher* had come under air attack from a Zeppelin and a German Sea plane, both of which had dropped bombs. Beatty now realised that the remaining German Battlecruisers had escaped and ordered the Squadron onto a course to re-join with HMS *Lion*, forming up with her at 2.00 pm, when he was informed that her starboard engine was suffering problems due to priming and that she would probably not be capable of steaming under her own power for at least 12-hours. This condition did not improve as time wore on and at 3.38 pm he ordered HMS *Indomitable* to take the *Lion* in tow, a task which was completed by 5.00 pm, with both Battlecruisers surrounded by Destroyers forming an anti-Submarine screen under Commodore (T), with the 2nd Light Cruiser Squadron having now rejoined, taking position S.E. 10 miles, and the 1st Light Cruiser Squadron taking position E. 10 miles, to provide a screen against the unlikely attack by enemy Destroyers.

HMS *Lion* arrived off May Island on the 26th. She was passed over from Indomitable to the tugs which had been dispatched from the Tyne while on passage from Inchkeith and *Lions* anchorage in the Forth, still escorted by elements of the Harwich Force. Beatty went back aboard the *Lion* when she was off May Island. As *Lion* proceeded up the Forth she was enveloped in a thick lying fog, through which could he heard loud cheers from crowds gathered on the Forth Bridge as the *Lion* approached the central span Island. In response *Lions* band was assembled on the 4-in gun deck and played "Rule Britannia".

With the injured *Lion* requiring dockyard time for repairs, Beatty transferred his Flag to *Princess Royal* and moved to this vessel along with his staff on the 27th.

Following the Dogger Bank action Captain Brock was promoted to Commodore and within four weeks promoted again to Rear-Admiral. Admiral Moore was promoted and moved from command of the 2nd Battle Cruiser Squadron to another post.

To say Lord Fisher, the First Sea Lord, was angry at the outcome of the battle is an understatement. He wrote a letter to Beatty asking why the action had been suddenly broken off. Beatty's reply was hand delivered to Fisher in London, to which Fisher apparently said to the courier "Well" to which he was handed Beatty's note. After reading the note of only a few lines he suddenly recognised that the messenger was someone from the *Lion* and he barked out "Well tell me about it. How was it that they got a way? What's the explanation? Why didn't you get the lot? And the *Derfflinger* I counted on her being sunk and we hear she got back practically unmolested. I don't understand it". *Derfflinger* had been damaged; it was the *Moltke* which had escaped without any significant damage. On hearing a technical and tactical explanation, including a scenario involving Submarines, Fisher retorted "Submarines? There weren't any. We know the position of every Submarine in the North Sea and there wasn't a mine within fifty miles".

Top: The major casualty of the Dogger bank action was SMS *Blucher*, here rolling onto her side with crew clambering over her hull. The Blucher was a large modern Armoured Cruiser, but operated with the Battle Cruisers of the Scouting Force. Above: When *Lion* dropped out of the British line due to heavy damage, Beatty transferred his flag to the Destroyer HMS *Attack*; here with Beatty on the Bridge.

Although figures vary slightly from document to document the following are considered accurate. HMS *Lion* sustained 18 hits, *Tiger* sustained 7 hits, *Indomitable* sustained 1 hit and *Princess Royal* and *New Zealand* were not hit. HMS *Lion* fired 180 x 13.5 in rounds, *Tiger* fired 400 x 13.5 in, *New Zealand* fired 141 x 12 in, and *Indomitable* fired 146 x 12 inch. The breakdown for the *New Zealand* was: 'A' Turret 15 rounds from right hand gun and 17 rounds from left gun; 'P' Turret 15 rounds from the right hand gun and 18 from the left hand gun; 'Q' Turret 14 rounds from right gun and 14 from the left gun; 'X' Turret 24 rounds from the right gun and 24 from the left gun.

The German Battlecruisers were in line *Derfflinger, Seydlitz, Moltke* and *Blucher*. Derfflinger sustained 3 x 13.4 in hits, Seydlitz was hit 3 times by 13.5 in shells from *Lion* and *Tiger*, and *Moltke* was not hit according to official documents. However, survivors from the Blucher in her rear claimed to have observed at least one hit on the Moltke. The Blucher was hit countless times; estimates vary from several times to well over 80. She was also hit by a at least one torpedo; some survivors stating two torpedo hits. Her casualties totalled over 800.

British

1st Battle Cruiser Squadron

HMS *Lion*
HMS *Princess Royal*
HMS *Tiger*

2nd Battle Cruiser Squadron

HMS *New Zealand*
HMS *Indomitable*

1st Light Cruiser Squadron

Destroyer Flotilla

German Battlecruisers

SMS Moltke
SMS Derfflinger
SMS Seydlitz
SMS Blucher (Modern Armoured Cruiser)

Light Cruisers and Torpedo Boat Destroyers

The Battle Cruiser Fleet

Going into February 1915, the 1st Battle Cruiser Squadron was at reduced strength as HMS *Lion* was still undergoing temporary repairs and HMS *Tiger* was refitting, leaving only HMS *Princess Royal* and *Queen Mary* active. The 2nd Battle Cruiser Squadron had only HMS *New Zealand* active as HMS *Indomitable* was undergoing a refit and repairs following a fire caused by faulty electric circuits.

February 1915 saw the Grand Fleet's Battlecruisers and Light Cruiser forces undergo a reorganization which saw the constitution of what became known as the Battle Cruiser Fleet, under the command of Vice-Admiral Beatty, with the title of Vice-Admiral Commanding the Battle Cruiser Fleet. This gave the false impression that the Battle Cruiser Fleet was a separate entity from the Grand Fleet, which it was not. It remained an integral part of the Grand Fleet under the overall command of Admiral Jellicoe. The Battle Cruiser Fleet was later renamed the more appropriate Battle Cruiser Force when Jellicoe moved to the Admiralty as First Sea Lord in the second half of 1916.

Based on Rosyth the Battle Cruiser Fleet consisted of the following assets:

HMS *Lion* continued in its capacity as Beatty's flagship, but was no longer part of the 1st Battle Cruiser Squadron, but now became the flagship of the Battle Cruiser Fleet.

The 1st Battle Cruiser Squadron consisted of HMS *Princess Royal* (Flagship of Rear-Admiral O. de B. Brock), HMS *Queen Mary* and HMS *Tiger*.

The 2nd Battle Cruiser Squadron consisted of HMAS *Australia* (Flagship of Rear-Admiral W. C. Pakenham), HMS *New Zealand* and HMS *Indefatigable*.

The 3rd Battle Cruiser Squadron consisted of HMS *Invincible* (designated as flagship), HMS *Inflexible* (*Inflexible* did not join the squadron until summer 1915 when she returned from the Mediterranean) and HMS *Indomitable*.

The 1st Light Cruiser Squadron consisted of HMS *Galatea* (flying the Broad pennant of Commodore E. S. Alexander-Sinclair), HMS *Cordelia*, HMS *Caroline* and HMS *Inconstant*.

The 2nd Light Cruiser Squadron consisted of HMS *Southampton* (flying the Broad pennant of Commodore W. E. Goodenough), HMS *Nottingham*, HMS *Birmingham* and HMS *Lowestoft*.

The 3rd Light Cruiser Squadron consisted of HMS *Falmouth* (Flagship of Rear-

Admiral Trevelyan Napier), HMS *Yarmouth*, HMS *Gloucester* and HMS *Liverpool*.

HMAS Australia officially joined the 2nd Battle Cruiser Squadron at Rosyth on 17 February and HMS *Indefatigable* joined the squadron on 24 February (some records show her joining the Squadron in March 1915) following her return from the Mediterranean.

HMS *Invincible* joined the 3rd Battle Squadron as Flagship at Rosyth in the early part of March.

On 1 February, HMS *Tiger* arrived on the Tyne where she entered refit, which was completed on the 8th, on which date she departed for Rosyth. Following her temporary repairs at Rosyth HMS *Lion* sailed for the Tyne, arriving on 9 February, where she remained for some time under repair, not returning to Rosyth until 7 April.

The Grand Fleet's Dreadnought Battle Squadrons conducted a cruise in the Northern area of the North Sea between 7 and 10 March accompanied by the 1st 2nd and 7th Cruiser Squadrons and the 4th Destroyer Flotilla. At the same time the newly constituted Battle Cruiser Fleet conducted a cruise in the central area of the North Sea.

British intelligence gathering, including German wireless intercepts, in late March indicated that the High Sea's Fleet was putting to sea. The Grand Fleet initiated its necessary, if predictable countermove and put to sea on 29 March, in the hope of intercepting the German Fleet and bringing it to battle. Wireless intercepts and Submarine reports noted that the German Fleet was returning to port on the night of 29 March, therefore, the Grand Fleet put about and returned to port.

The Battle Cruiser Fleet, along with eight Destroyers from the 1st Flotilla, conducted a cruise in the northern North Sea between 5 and 9 April, while the 3rd Battle Squadron, the 3rd Cruiser Squadron and five Destroyers, also from the 1st Flotilla, conducted a cruise in the central area of the North Sea between 5 and 8 April.

The main body of the Grand Fleet put to sea on 11 April with the Dreadnought Battle Fleet rendezvousing with the Rosyth based Battle Cruiser Fleet, the 3rd Battle Squadron and the 3rd Cruiser Squadron, to conduct a cruise in the central North Sea during the course of 12 and 13 April, before the fleet returned to its respective bases on the 14th in order to refuel.

The above sorties were no doubt conducted in response to intelligence report of enemy intentions. In early April, the German Fleet had planned to mount an operation to sow a minefield at the Swarte Bank (an area of the North Sea, which lies about 100 miles from the mouth of the River Humber). This operation was to be covered by a powerful naval force consisting of most of the High Sea's Fleet. Again, the British intelligence machine had deciphered signals giving the Grand Fleet advance warning of the intended German sortie. Concerned that the Germans may begin to suspect that their codes had been broken if the Grand Fleet suddenly continually put to sea shortly after the German Fleet, the Admiralty decided that the Grand Fleet would actually sail prior to the Germans leaving port.

The Germans first conducted a reconnaissance of the intended operational area under the supervision of Admiral Von Pohl, with Zeppelins being the main tool utilised for this purpose. The Zeppelins reported that a British Light Cruiser Squadron, supported by Destroyers and Submarines, had been sighted near Terschelling on an easterly course. The German High Command concluded that the British Fleet was preparing an attack of its own and the German operation was, therefore, postponed.

The Dreadnought Battle Fleet proceeded to sea at 08:00 am on 17 April, screened by the 1st, 2nd and 7th Cruiser squadrons out in front, with the 2nd and 4th Destroyer Flotillas providing an anti-Submarine screen. The fleet proceeded south; heading for position Latitude 56.30 N., Longitude 3.30 E., for a rendezvous with the Rosyth based 3rd Battle Squadron and 3rd Cruiser squadron, which were met at 4:00 pm, with the Battle Cruiser Fleet also arriving in the vicinity of the fleet at this time from its previous position slightly further to the south.

These sailings were conducted in response to the German mine laying operation, which following further delays due to weather consideration (mostly fog), was eventually conducted on 17 April, which had prompted the Admiralty to order the above noted fleet movements.

The Admiralty was able to monitor the movements of the German Fleet; however, it remained in the dark as to the precise nature of the operation. Through the night the Grand Fleet sailed south easterly and by midday on the 18th was half way across the North Sea, heading for the Danish Coast. Beatty's Battle Cruiser Fleet was steaming some seventy miles south east of the Grand Fleet.

The British effort to intercept the German force was in vein, however, as the operation had already been conducted with the German Light Cruisers SMS *Stralsund* and *Strassburg* laying the new minefield during the course of the night of the 17th and the early hours of the 18th. By the time the Grand Fleet was in the above noted position the German High Sea's Fleet was already well on its way back to port, having turned back early on the morning of the 18th. None of the Grand Fleet heavy units, including the Battlecruisers, had got close to the German Fleet, with only the Destroyers of the Harwich force being in the

General vicinity of the German operation. Even this force, however, failed to locate any German vessels or even Zeppelin Scout Airships.

There was no sign of enemy activity and the fleet turned northward just before dusk on the 18th, at which point it was in the area of the 'The Little Fisher Bank', which is located to the west of Northern Denmark.

During the course of the night, the 3rd Battle Squadron, in company with the 3rd Cruiser Squadron, was ordered to detach and return to Rosyth. The 2nd and 4th Destroyer Flotillas were ordered to Scapa and the Battle Fleet and 1st, 2nd and 7th Cruiser Squadrons headed for an area to the eastward of the Shetlands in order to conduct gunnery practice, returning to Scapa and Cromarty during the night of 20/21 April. The Battle Cruiser Fleet was ordered to continue the southern cruise through the 19th.

The see-saw motion of the High Sea's Fleet putting to sea and the Grand Fleet sailing to counter continued on 21 April when a claimed 21 German Dreadnoughts (this figure could only have been accurate if it included Battlecruisers as well as Battleships), 12 Light Cruisers and 52 Destroyers. This sortie had very limited objectives of isolating and destroying British Light forces patrols in the area of the Dogger Bank. During the morning of 22 April, leading German forces were approaching close to the Dogger Bank. However, the Zeppelin Scouts operating ahead of the German ships reported no signs of British vessels in the area, with the exception of a lone British Trawler, which was sunk by the Germans.

The Grand Fleet had sailed during the night of 21 April from its bases at Scapa and Cromarty to conduct a sweep of the North Sea towards the coast of Denmark in the hope of intercepting the German Fleet off the mouth of the Skagerrak. The force comprised the 1st, 2nd and 4th Battle Squadrons, the 1st, 2nd and 7th Cruiser Squadrons and the pre-Dreadnoughts HMS *Russell* and HMS *Albemarle*; these two vessels, which had arrived at Scapa on the 19th to conduct target practice were from the 6th Battle Squadron, but had only recently moved to join the 3rd Battle Squadron at Rosyth from their previous posting to the Channel Fleet. The heavy ships were screened by the 2nd and 4th Destroyer Flotillas. At 4.30 pm, the main Battle Fleet was joined by the 3rd Battle Squadron and the 3rd Cruiser Squadron from Rosyth and the Battle Cruiser Fleet was positioned ahead of the Battle Fleets Cruiser screen.

By dusk, the Battle Fleet was in position Latitude 57.11 N., Longitude 4.53 E., (Flagship *Iron Duke's* position) and as no enemy vessels had been encountered. Again the British had been frustrated as the German Fleet had returned to port when it failed to locate British light forces. The British plan to intercept the German Fleet had also included the dispatch of Submarines to the Heligoland Bight in the hope of being able to attack the German ships as they returned to port. However, the Submarines were not in position before the Germans were safely back in port.

Admiral Jellicoe ordered the fleet to turn northward. The Battle Cruiser Fleet, along with the 3rd Battle Squadron and 3rd Cruiser Squadron, detached from the main fleet and returned to Rosyth, while the Battle Fleet returned to Scapa and Cromarty during the course of the 23rd.

The strength of the Grand Fleet was increased with the arrival of the new *Queen Elizabeth* Class Super Dreadnought fast Battleship HMS *Warspite* at Scapa Flow on 13 April. The *Queen Elizabeth* Class were the most powerful warships afloat at the time. Heavily armed and heavily armoured, they fast; with a speed f 25 knots they were almost as fast as the first generation Battlecruisers.

During April 1915, HMS *Invincible* detached from the Battle Cruiser Fleet and proceeded to the Tyne so some of her 12-in guns could be changed as they were worn following her service in the South Atlantic the previous December.

This routine continued in May when the German High Sea's Fleet sailed on the 17th to support a mine laying operation in the Dogger Bank. Shortly after the Germans left port, the Grand Fleet was ordered to sea on the morning of the 17th, but was ordered to return the following day when it became clear that the German Fleet had returned to port.

The fleet units at sea between 17 and 19 May, the Grand Fleet conducted a sweep of the central area of the North Sea. The various elements of the fleet, sailing from their bases at Scapa, Cromarty and Rosyth, rendezvoused at 07.00 am on the 18th, with the Battle Cruiser Fleet taking station between thirty and fifty miles ahead of the Battle Fleet as the sweep was conducted on a south-eastward course at a speed of 16 knots. Without encountering any German warships the various elements of the fleet returned to their respective bases on the 19th.

The Grand Fleet received the news that Italy had entered the war on the Allied side in a telegraph from the Admiralty on 24 May 1915, although this news would do nothing to effect the operations in the North Sea.

Admiral Sir Henry Jackson succeeded Lord Fisher as First Sea Lord in May 1915, when the latter dramatically resigned his position as First Sea Lord following the scandal of the Gallipoli debacle. Jellicoe went to Rosyth in HMS *Iron Duke* for a conference with the new First Sea Lord on 25 May, with the meeting taking place on the 26th. On this day, the Flag of Rear-Admiral the Hon. Horace Hood C.B., was hoisted on HMS *Invincible* as Flagship of the 3rd Battle Cruiser Squadron, and the 15-in gun Super Dreadnought *Queen Elizabeth* Class Battleship HMS *Queen Elizabeth* arrived at Scapa Flow following her service at the Dardanelles, adding significantly to the strength of the Grand Fleet.

As the German mine laying operations continued, so too did the High Sea's Fleet operations to support them. On 29 May, the High Sea's Fleet sailed as a diversion to cover the breakout of an armed Mine Layer. This prompted the countermove by the British, and the Grand Fleet sailed on the night of the 29th, on the now familiar easterly course, so the Rosyth based Battle Cruiser Fleet could rendezvous with the Grand Fleet, before turning south east in the hope of intercepting the German Fleet. When the Germans headed back to port, the Admiralty recalled the Grand Fleet. This familiar pattern was now beginning to receive attention from the Germans who were noting the sailings of the Grand Fleet shortly after theirs followed by the turnaround of the British following the German turn for port. The coincidences of these apparent shadow movements seemed too much and from this point onwards the Germans were in little doubt that the British were receiving information as to the movements of the German Fleet, although they were convinced that it was being passed on through a network of spies and not through wireless intercepts.

The Grand Fleet units that had sailed on the 29th conducted a sweep in the North Sea towards the Dogger Bank between that date and 31st May. The Battle Fleet, Cruisers and Destroyers departed from Scapa and Cromarty, meeting in position Latitude 57.35 N., Longitude 0.0 at 07.15 am on 30 May, and then proceeded on southerly course to join the Rosyth based elements which were proceeding to an area further to the south, being in sight of the Battle Fleets Cruiser screen at 9.30 am. With the Rosyth based Squadrons out ahead, the Sweep continued south until the Battle Fleet was in the general area of the Dogger Bank, before swinging northward as no enemy warships were encountered. At night the Rosyth Squadrons detached and returned to base and the main fleet headed for its northern bases arriving during the morning of the 31st.

By the end of May the Germans had completed their planned mine laying operations resulting in June being a month of relative inactivity in so far as Fleet size operations were concerned. This had the result that the Grand Fleet became less active and is only recorded as having put to see on a fleet scale on one occasion during the month, this being to conduct fleet and firing exercises on the 11th, which included the involvement of the Rosyth, based Battle Cruiser Force.

On 11 June 1915, the Grand Fleet departed from its various anchorages to conduct the cruise in northern waters. The main aim of this cruise as was to conduct gunnery exercises and battle tactics. These exercises were notable in that it was the first time in history that Sea Planes would work with Royal Navy large surface units. The Sea Planes were operated from the Sea Plane Carrier HMS *Campania*, and these exercises would be the beginnings of the Grand Fleets program of including aircraft operating with the main fleet, which would later see aircraft operated from flying off platforms on Battleships, Battlecruisers and other vessels leading to the eventual development of the Aircraft Carrier, which would be a major element of the Fleet, particularly in the last year of the war.

The Battle Fleet sailed from Scapa and Cromarty and conducted gunnery exercises against targets towed by Colliers to the westward of the Shetlands during the course of 12 June. During the evening of the 12th, the Battle Fleet separated to conduct night firing exercises. The Rosyth based Battle Cruiser Fleet also conducted night firing exercises during the 12th, before the fleet joined up again to conduct battle exercises during the 13th. Following this the Battle Cruiser Fleet conducted gunnery exercises, firing on targets towed by the Colliers, before rendezvousing with the Battle Fleet on the morning of the 14th. There followed further battle exercises, again utilising the Sea Planes from the *Campania* for scouting, before the fleet fragmented and returned to their respective bases.

The Rosyth based 3rd Battle Squadron, 3rd Cruiser Squadron and half of the 1st Destroyer Flotilla were not present during the exercises as they were conducting a cruise in the central area of the North Sea.

HMS *Inflexible* arrived at Rosyth from Gibraltar on 19 June joining the 3rd Battle Cruiser Squadron.

Grand Fleet 30 May 1915

Dreadnought and Super Dreadnought Battleships	25
Pre-Dreadnought Battleships	10
Battle Cruisers	9
Armoured Cruisers	17
Light Cruisers (Modern)	26
Flotilla Leaders	5
Destroyers (modern)	93
Destroyers (old)	15
Armed Merchant Cruisers	24
Armed Boarding Steamers	8

Warships station in home waters, which were not part of the Grand Fleet

Pre-Dreadnought Battleships	4
Armoured Cruisers	1
Destroyers (new modern)	13
Destroyers (old)	81
Torpedo boats (oil burning)	36
Submarines	65
Monitors	3
(These were allocated for transfer to the Mediterranean)	
Sloops	1
Armed boarding steamers	12

7

THE FIRST DARDANELLES BOMBARDMENT – NOVEMBER 1914

Although Turkey was not a belligerent nation, following the *Goeben* and *Breslau's* arrival in the safety of Turkish anchorages, the Admiralty decided to set up a permanent presence of warships off the Dardanelles to keep watch on the entrance to the straits lest the *Goeben* and *Breslau* suddenly re-appear in the Mediterranean flying German colours again. This operation, which soon became known as the Dardanelles patrol, utilised many elements of the British Mediterranean Fleet with French support, although the French were actually in overall command in the Mediterranean theatre. Among the ships embarking upon these patrols was a trio of Destroyers from a sub-Division of the 5th Destroyer Flotilla led by the *Beagle* Class Destroyer HMS *Harpy*, with the British setting up base at Syra. The British Battlecruisers, which had pursued the *Goeben* to the Dardanelles, were available in case she came back out, or in case Turkey entered the war on the German side.

Even though the Allies and Turkey were not at war, some officers were suggesting bold plans for attacking the warships in Turkish waters. This included a suggested "dash up the Dardanelles" put forward by Captain Dickens in the *Harpy*.

The British Naval Mission under the command of Rear-Admiral Limpus, which was tasked with assisting Turkey with the modernisation of its navy, was recalled to Britain on 14 September 1914, effectively severing Britain's naval association with Turkey. This move probably instilled a feeling in the Turkish Military and Political circles that Britain may have been preparing for war against Turkey due to the latter's links with Germany. Turkey Officially closed the Dardanelle's on 3 October 1914, probably in response to the British Squadron of Warships, which had effectively set up station outside the Straits following the pursuit of the *Goeben* and *Breslau* in early August.

On 29 October, Turkish warships conducted a raid against Odessa, and the following day the *Breslau* bombarded Theodosia and Novorissik. These acts of war against Russia, Britain and France's Triple Entente ally against the Central Powers, effectively meant war against Britain and France was at most a few days away. On 1 November, the staff of the Allied Consuls began leaving Constantinople further signaling the likelihood of a war, which was declared on November. The very same day the Turkish Gun-Boat *Burak Reis* was sunk just off Smyrna and the following day the Allied squadron on station off the Dardanelles moved into position to threaten the straits.

The Dardanelles. UK NA

On 3 November 1914, British warships including the Battlecruisers, *Indefatigable* and *Indomitable* and the Destroyer *Harpy* conducted a 20 minute bombardment of the Turkish forts positioned at the entrance to the Narrows. However, this was not followed up by subsequent bombardments and the only other engagement between Turkish fort guns and British warships was when a fort gun fired a single shot at HMS *Harpy*, which had steamed too close inshore.

Following the Dardanelle's bombardment success was initially much exaggerated, with some claims that the a huge explosions had ripped through Fort Helle's producing huge plumes of thick smoke and even that the *Goeben* had been damaged while lying in the Straits. There would have been explosions in Fort Helle's when shells burst, but in truth, not too much in the way of damage had been done and certainly nothing of great tactical or strategic value.

The bombardment had achieved nothing of strategically important value and the slight damage done to fort installations could easily be made good by the Turks. The bombardment itself came in for much criticism as there was no objective other than lobbing a few shells at Turkish forts simply to make the presence of the Allied ships known. Of course, their presence was already known. Putting invaluable, in the case of the Battlecruisers, hard, if not impossible to replace, ships at risk for such a futile bombardment would on studying the strategic situation at that time seem nothing short of reckless incompetence. Even moderate damage to one or both of the Battlecruisers would have temporarily caused a serious reduction in the British Battlecruiser strength, particularly at a time when it had become apparent that they were urgently needed, particularly in the North Sea. The events at Coronel off the Pacific coast of Chile on 1 November when Admiral Cradock squadron had been destroyed by Von Spees' squadron would lead to a decision to send the *Inflexible* and *Invincible* to the South Atlantic. The German bombardment of British East Coast towns by Battlecruisers and Light Cruisers on 3 November 1914 demonstrated the requirement for Battlecruisers in the North Sea as none of the Dreadnought Battleships were fast enough to catch the German Battlecruisers if they repeated their attacks on British East Coast. In retrospect, it seems that the main beneficiary of the bombardment was Turkey itself, which if it was not already so, was abruptly awakened to the potential vulnerability of its fort defences to the Dardanelles and of the Allies interest in it as a strategic point. This allowed Turkey to speed up and extend its already planned program of strengthening the defences, which would tell against the Anglo-French fleet that attempted to force the Dardanelles a few months later.

The 3rd of November 1914 also saw a bombardment take place against the Turkish defences on the town of Akaba by the old *Eclipse* Class protected Cruiser HMS *Minerva*, with support from the Destroyers HMS *Savage* and *Scorpion*, followed by a landing to oust the Turkish garrison, which was under the command of a German Officer. A further bombardment of Smyrna took place on 7 November. Churchill lobbied for a second bombardment of the Dardanelles Forts to be conducted on 16 November, but this was overruled.

8

HMS *INFLEXIBLE* AT THE DARDANELLES AND AFTER - FEBRUARY TO JUNE 1915

On 14 February 1915, orders were issued for the strategic plan to force the Dardanelle's. The basic orders were for the Anglo-French Fleet to force a passage through the Dardanelle's Straits into the Sea of Marmora, reduce the enemy defences, ranging from the mouth of the straits up to Nagara and to clear all minefields. The plan called for the Turkish forts guarding the Dardanelles to be bombarded by the fleet at long-range, with direct or indirect fire from the Battleship main batteries, to try and silence the enemy 24-cm L/22 and 35-cm L/35 guns, which it was expected had effective ranges of around 10,000 and 12,000 yards respectively. Once these were silenced the Battleships could move into close range and employ their secondary batteries. There was no requirement for salvo firing as would be the norm when engaging an enemy Battle fleet.

The plan was to be implemented in seven main phases, which were **1.** Reduction of the defences at the entrance to the Dardanelle's. **2.** Sweep any minefields and reduction of the defences as far as the Narrows. **3.** Silencing the forts at the Narrows, **4.** Sweeping any minefields encountered in the Narrows. **5.** Silencing the forts located above the Narrows. **6.** The passage of the Anglo-French fleet into the Sea of Marmora, **7.** Conduct operations in the Sea of Marmora and conduct patrols off the Dardanelle's.

To implement the plan the Royal Navy wanted additional heavy ships to augment those already in the Mediterranean. It was particularly desirable to have as modern ships as they could for the first line which would try and force the Dardanelle's. The Battlecruiser HMS *Inflexible* was already in the Mediterranean, along with the relatively modern pre-Dreadnought Battleship HMS *Lord Nelson*, which was very heavily armed with four 12-in guns of the same model as those found on the first generation of British Dreadnoughts, and a battery of 10 x BL 9.2-in MK XI guns. With this fire-power they were at least a match for the first generation Battlecruisers then in service, albeit much slower, and could in concert with other warships be used to counter the *Goeben*, which was the only heavy Turkish ship capable of seriously interfering with operations in the Dardanelles. However, while heavily armed and armoured, with a maximum speed of 19 knots she lacked the speed to catch the *Goeben* if she chose to run. This in part was *Inflexible's* reason for being transferred to the Eastern Mediterranean after she returned from the Falklands Battle.

Although adequate assets were in place to counter the *Goeben*, additional assets were still desired to beef up the bombardment force of old French and British pre-Dreadnought Battleships, which was now assembling for the Dardanelles operation. HMS *Lord Nelsons* sister ship, HMS *Agamemnon* departed Britain on 9 February 1915, bound for Malta, where she arrived to coal on the 15th, before continuing on to the Island of Tenedos in the Northern Aegean Sea, leaving Malta in the late afternoon of the 16th with orders to rendezvous with the *Queen Elizabeth Class* Battleship HMS *Queen Elizabeth* the following morning off Filfla Island, 5 kilometers south of Malta. The *Queen Elizabeth*, which was a brand new Super Dreadnought Battleship armed with a main battery of 8 x 15-in guns, damaged one of her turbines and *Agamemnon* was sent to escort her to Tenedos, arriving on the 19th.

Around 3,30 pm on 19 February, HMS *Agamemnon*, with HMS *Queen Elizabeth* following some miles astern of her, arrived to join the Allied Fleet of the Dardanelles. A number of the Allied Battleships were already engaging the forts and *Agamemnon* was ordered to close up on the Flagship of the fleet, HMS *Inflexible*, and take position two cables to seaward from her, arriving on station at 4.10 pm in the afternoon. At this time, the pre-Dreadnought Battleship HMS *Vengeance* was bombarding No.4 fort close to Kum Kale, while HMS *Cornwallis* was firing on the fort at Seddul Bahr. The order of bombardment was being controlled from the *Inflexible* and at 5.00 pm *Agamemnon* received a signal from *Inflexible* ordering her to support HMS *Cornwallis*. *Agamemnon* closed up to a range of around 7,000 yards from No.3 fort at Cape Helles and commenced her bombardment. *Inflexible* signaled the fleet to cease firing and retire at 5.20 pm, after which the ships proceeded on a course taking them between Sigri, near the western end of Lesbos Island, and Tenedos to spend the night.

On the 5th of March HMS *Queen Elizabeth* was to anchor off Gaba Tape so as to provide a steady gun platform to increase accuracy for her 15-in guns, which would engage No.13, 17 and 20 forts by firing over the Peninsula, with a ship inside the straits spotting for her. A number of vessels were tasked with providing cover for her against firing from mobile batteries on the shore. Among these was the Pre-Dreadnought Battleship HMS *Prince George* with *HMS Inflexible* in close support, as well as Destroyers. When a battery very close to the shore opened fire on the *Queen Elizabeth*, hitting her with their first salvo, the *Prince George* moved to engage it, finding it quite difficult to locate as it was behind a low hill. The *Queen Elizabeth* was hit again before the *Prince George* commenced firing on the suspected location. Unclear as to whether or not the battery had been hit the *Prince George* took solace in the fact that it did not fire on the *Queen Elizabeth* again, which had not been seriously damaged, although she had been hit a number times, including a direct hit in the wardroom. The suspected position of the Turkish battery was then engaged by *HMS Inflexible's* 4-in secondary battery as well as *Queen Elizabeth's* 6-in secondary battery. *Queen Elizabeth* continued to engage the forts by firing over the Peninsula throughout the afternoon before the force retired back to Tenedos around 6.00 pm.

On 10 March the Commander in Chief transferred his Flag from HMS *Inflexible* to the *Queen Elizabeth*. *Inflexible* then proceeded to Malta on the same date in order that she could replace two of her 12-in guns which were worn out due to heavy use in the Battle of the Falkland Islands in December 1914, and then in Dardanelles bombardments.

HMS *Canopus* bombards Turkish positions in the Dardanelles in March 1915.

On the Morning of 18 March, the Minesweeping operation reported that the Dardanelles had been effectively cleared of any mines, at least up to a distance of around 8,000 yards of the forts at the Narrows. This report effectively indicated that the area where the Anglo-French warships would be initially operating was safe from the risk of mines. However, unbeknown to the Anglo-

French commanders, on 8 March a mine belt of twenty moored mines had been laid more or less parallel to the shoreline of Erin Keui Bay by the Turkish Navy Minelayer *Nousret*. The logic behind the Turks choosing this particular area to lay the small minefield was that British warships had been noted to be operating in this area during one of the previous Dardanelle's sorties. Under the belief that the area was clear of mines, the Anglo-French command assumed that the fort guns would be the main problem to their warships navigating the Dardanelles the following day.

Turkish 11 inch heavy gun position at the Dardanelles.

On 18 March the Allied Fleet entered the Dardanelles Straits at 10.00 am, preceded by the River Class Destroyer HMS *Chelmer* and the Destroyer HMS *Colne* and the Battleships picket boats. The *Colne* was equipped with a minesweeping suite and steamed to make a fast sweep to check the area before the Battleship Line 'A' proceeded to their designated firing positions.

The first line of ships, Line A, consisted of the heavy squadron, HMS *Queen Elizabeth*, the two powerful pre-Dreadnought Battleships HMS *Lord Nelson* and HMS *Agamemnon* and HMS *Inflexible*, now returned from Malta. *Queen Elizabeth*, with her powerful battery of eight 15-in guns, was tasked with engaging targets on the Northern or European shore, whilst the *Inflexible*, *Lord Nelson* and *Agamemnon*, with their 12-in main batteries, would engage the southern or Asian shore.

Top: The Pre-Dreadnought Battleship HMS *Agamemnon* fires her secondary battery of 9.2 inch guns at Turkish fortifications at Sedd el Bahr on 4 March 1915. *Agamemnon* was a powerful ship, with a main battery of four 12 inch guns of the same type used by the first British Dreadnoughts including the Invincible and Indefatigable Class Battlecruisers. Above: HMS *Inflexible* fires her forward 12 inch guns at Turkish fortifications at the Dardanelles.

Each of the Battleships and the Battlecruiser *Inflexible* were allocated a steamboat manned by their respective crews to deal with mines that could be encountered inside the Straits. The ships proceeded to a range of around 14,000 yards from the Narrows. The flanks of the heavy squadron were covered by the old pre-Dreadnought Battleships HMS *Triumph* and *Prince George* with a squadron of four old French pre-Dreadnought Battleships, *Suffren, Bouvet, Gaulois* and *Charlemange,* behind the heavy squadron with orders to pass through the squadron in the event the forts were successfully silenced.

Prior to Line 'A' opening fire the ships had come under very light and ineffective artillery fire from a few shore positions. At 11.25 am the *Queen Elizabeth* opened fire on the forts on her side, while *Lord Nelson, Agamemnon* and *Inflexible* were each to engage a fort on their side, with *Lord Nelson* allocated No.17 fort and *Inflexible* tasked with engaging No.13 fort. *Inflexible* and the two *Lord Nelson Class* ships opened fire around 11.35 am.

In order to increase accuracy the ships had stopped when firing commenced making them easier targets for Turkish guns returning fire. All four ships were subjected to a fierce storm of fire from shore based Howitzers and it was only luck on their part and poor aiming on the Turkish part that all the ships did not suffer severe damage. The fire directed at *Inflexible* seemed to be more accurate, mainly due to the fact that she was positioned fairly close below the Village of Aren Kioi, which had previously been identified as being a position well endowed with Turkish Howitzers. This type of position proved to be more of a problem for the Allied ships than the larger forts, which proved to be easily silenced. The defenders were obviously aware that most of the Allied fleet's attention would be directed at the main forts and relied to an extent on mobile and static concealed Howitzer batteries to engage the Allied Battleships. The main forts appeared to be silent less than an hour after the *Queen Elizabeth* opened fire, allowing the older French Battleships to proceed ahead and engage them at closer range.

Around noon, *Queen Elizabeth* was engaging the fort at Chanak when it was assumed the forts magazine had blown up as there was a terrible explosion. Around this time, HMS *Inflexible* was engaging No.13 fort on the Asiatic coast. *Inflexible* luck ran out around 12.15 pm when she was struck on the roof of the foretop, killing or wounding most of the occupants within, with only two men apparently unhurt. Both of the Officers, Commander Verner and Lieutenant Blaker were badly wounded, and both succumbed to their wounds that evening. Crew onboard the *Prince George* observed the shell hit on the *Inflexible* foretop and observed the Bridge to be on fire. Eventually *Prince George*, which had also received two hits, engaged No.13 fort with her 12-in battery before switching fire to No.9 fort. *Inflexible* was noted to fall out of the line after being struck and damaged. Once she had a fire brought under control she rejoined Line 'A', which then regained its integrity.

The actions continued for several hours with a number of the ships in the advance line being hit, although none suffered serious damage. The four French Battleships were relieved by four British pre- Dreadnoughts and then began to retire back down the straits. Things started to go very badly at 2.00 pm when the old French Pre-Dreadnought Battleship *Bouvet* struck a mine while returning back down the straits at high speed in the Aren Kioi Bay, the damage of which resulted in an internal explosion, which destroyed the ship and caused her to capsize and sink in around two minutes with only around 37 survivors. Despite the loss of the *Bouvet*, the Allied Force continued its slow advance up the Straits, but suffered another major setback when the *Inflexible* shook and shuddered as she struck a mine around 4.05 pm to 4.11 pm (reported times vary) as she moved through the area of Erin Keui Bay, by which time the advance ships had reached a point some five miles from the entrance to the Straits. "We felt a frightful shock and the whole ship shook and rocked. I thought it was a mine and went up to the next deck to see what was up. Shortly, there sounded the 'clear lower deck bugle' and then one came running everyone on deck'… Of course the poor wounded had to be man-handled in no very gentle fashion to get them up on deck quickly". Fleet Paymaster Henry Horniman Royal Navy.

Inflexible sustained serious damage resulting in the forward torpedo room flooding. The hole caused by the mine was located in her submerged flat, forward, being some 40-ft x 30-ft in area. After making it out of the straits, *Inflexible* anchored a short distance from HMS *Amethyst* in shoal water.

In the aftermath of hitting the mine Lieutenant-Commander Acheson, along with Acting Sub-Lieutenant Alfred E. B. Giles, Chief E R A 2nd Class Robert Snowdon O N 270654 and Stoker 1st Class Thomas Davidson O N K 14753, proceeded to the forward magazine and shell room of *Inflexible* after the working parties previously in these area's had been forced out by severe fumes caused by the mine explosion beneath the ship. They managed to shut off valves and close watertight doors, working with the lights out and the shell room flooded with some 2 feet of water, which was continuing to slowly rise. Although affected by the fumes the party remained on station until ordered out by Lieutenant-Commander Acheson who was the last to leave. At the time *Inflexible* was proceeding to Tenedos with the engine room in "semi-darkness" as well as being very hot and the ship was in danger of foundering while en-route to Tenedos

Before *Inflexible* had her unfortunate encounter with the mine, her attendant picket boat had also been lost. On 18 March, Acting Sub-Lieutenant George Tothill Philip from *Inflexible* was in command of the Picket Boat tasked with dealing with floating mines. Under fire from shore batteries the Picket Boat was hit by a heavy artillery shell causing considerable damage. Philip maneuvered her alongside *Inflexible* and ordered his crew onboard before proceeding to the Picket Boat engine room to shut off the steam and then "closed scuttle to stockhold" before he too abandoned the boat.

While HMS *Inflexible* managed to stay afloat, the Pre-Dreadnought Battleship HMS *Irresistible* was not so lucky. This view from HMS *Lord Nelson* shows the *Irresistible* sinking in the Dardanelles.

The day's losses were not over yet as the Pre-Dreadnought Battleship HMS *Irresistible* struck a mine, which detonated under her bilge keel as she was drifting with her engines stopped. The Pre-Dreadnought Battleship HMS *Ocean* stood by *Irresistible* when at 5.50 pm it became clear she could not be saved and the order was given to abandon ship. Among the killed on the *Inflexible* had been the gunnery commander, therefore, the gunnery commander from the sunken HMS *Irresistible* was eventually sent to *Inflexible*.

Initial plans for the Allied Battleship force to remain within the Straits after darkness fell were hurriedly reviewed as it became painfully clear that it would have to be withdrawn to the Mediterranean side of the Straits due to the threat of mines, which was vastly increased in the hours of darkness.

The recall order was issued to the fleet with the flags hoisted. However, the days loss's were far from over as HMS *Ocean*, which had assisted HMS *Irresistible*, herself struck a mine at 6.05 pm and almost simultaneously she was hit by a shell from a shore gun, which damaged her steering gear, putting it out of action. Unable to steer and suffering serious damage from the mine explosion HMS *Ocean* was abandoned at 7.30 pm and both *Ocean* and *Irresistible* eventually sank during the course of the night. The huge losses of three Pre-Dreadnought Battleships (2 British and 1 French) and a damaged Battlecruiser in an area of water previously thought to have been clear of mines after an operation by Allied Minesweepers was a shock to the Naval Planners at the time. The mines actually came from a line of only 20 mines, which had been sown, on 8 March, down the line of advance down the Straits rather than across the Straits as would have been expected. This resulted in the Minesweepers missing then during their sweep of the channel.

The mines however, were not the only success for the enemy on that day against the combined Allied Fleet. A number of ships suffered shell fire damage and although most was not serious, two French Pre-Dreadnought Battleships suffered such extensive damage that they were effectively withdrawn from the Campaign and released from the operation to enter dockyard hands for repairs.

Badly damaged, *Inflexible* managed to move to Mudros under her own steam on 21 March. She then waited there for temporary repairs to be carried out to allow her to sail to Malta. These temporary repairs included an "elastic pad" covering the huge hole left by the mine explosion. The pad was constructed after a telegraph to Malta prompted the dispatch of a repair crew from the British Base. At Malta she would enter dry-dock and have new plates fitted, but the temporary patch was required to enable her to reach Malta. By 29 March, *Inflexible* had her temporary patch fitted at Mudros and had on this day finished pumping out her flooded compartments. Twelve of the unaccounted for crew were found dead and removed from the submerged flat were they had been when the mine exploded. That afternoon the men were buried at sea. Augmenting the temporary patch was a wood and cement bulkhead, which was built in place as a precaution against the patch losing its watertight integrity during her passage to Malta.

The venerable pre-Dreadnought Battleship HMS *Canopus* was allocated to escort *Inflexible* part of the way to Malta, before meeting the troopship *Alexandria*, which was transporting a Royal Navy Division to Skydros on Trebuki Island. *Canopus* arrived at Mudros on 3-4 April to coal before she and *Inflexible* sailed for Malta, both departing on the evening of 4 April, after a delay due to a gale blowing, with the ships awaiting a slackening of the high winds. The bad weather began improving on 7 April, however, *Inflexible* had encountered problems as her pumps had packed in and she was taking on water again. *Inflexible* dire position saw *Canopus* ordered to continue with her all the way to Malta. *Canopus* continued other duties while escorting *Inflexible*. She pursued and eventually stopped an American Archipelago Co. ship, which was suspected of carrying arms to the enemy. This ship was dispatched to Mudros for further examination.

On 8 April, work parties had improved the situation on *Inflexible* and she was capable of steaming at 8 knots. However, the following day, while still some 50 miles out from Malta, she was in some difficulty as the weather had again turned bad with another gale blowing. Her patch was failing and she was taking on so much water that she was unable to make any real headway against the gale force winds. In the rough sea *Inflexible* was in serious trouble and her Captain and the Captain of *Canopus* agreed on a plan to attempt to turn her around stern onto the wind, thereafter the *Canopus* would take her under tow with the *Inflexible* steaming full steam astern. Despite *Inflexible* poor condition, the high winds and rough sea, this task was successfully completed and the *Canopus*, with *Inflexible* in tow, eventually arrived off Malta not long before dark, with tugs coming out from Malta to assist *Inflexible* into port, where she was docked for repairs.

Following her repairs at Malta, HMS *Inflexible* sailed Gibraltar before returning to home waters, arriving at Rosyth on the River Forth n 19 June joining the 3rd Battle Cruiser Squadron.

APPENDICES

Appendix I

Invincible Class

Length: 567-ft (172.8-m) overall; 530 ft 0.75 in pp (*Inflexible* 530 ft 1 in pp and *Indomitable* 530 ft 1.75 in pp)

Beam: 78-ft 6-in (23.9-m) designed. Could vary a few inches from ship to ship

Draught: normal 25-ft (7.6-m) and deep 29-ft 7-in (9-m)

Displacement: design weight was 17,250 tons normal and 20,420 tons full deep load (deep displacement)

Fuel capacity: coal; 1000 tons of coal at load draught, 3000 tons of coal maximum; oil 700 tons

Speed: design speed of 25.5 knots, although all three vessels of the *Invincible* Class exceeded this during trials and in service

Armour Protection: armour belt 6-in thick amidships tapering to 4-in forward (The belt extended to 4 ft below and 7 ft 3 in above the low water line); barbets were 2-7-in (50-180-mm), main armament turrets were 7-in (180-mm), conning tower 6 to 10-in (150 to 250-mm) and communications tubes between 3 and 4 in with 2 in on lower control tower. The main deck was 0.75-in forward with lower deck 1.5 in forward, 2 in sloping amidships and 2.5 in aft; 1-2 in below 'A', 'P' and 'Q' main armament barbets with base having 2 in and 2.5 in anti-torpedo bulkheads (abreast of magazines only).

Armament: a main battery of eight 12-in/45 caliber Mk X guns in four turrets – one forward, one aft and one on each of the wings; 80 rounds per gun carried. As designed the secondary armament consisted of 18 x 12 pdr guns, but this was altered to 16 x 4-in (102-mm)/45 Caliber QF (Quick Firing) guns as built. The class was built with 5 x 18 in (457 mm) submerged torpedo tubes. Additional armament included up to 7 x Maxim machine guns and a number of small arms

Complement: As designed 704, increased to 755 as built, but normal complement was around 784, although this increased to over 1,000 during World War 1

Appendix II

Indefatigable Class

Length: 590-ft (180-m) overall; 555 ft pp design (Indefatigable 555 ft 0.25 in pp; New Zealand 555 ft 1 in pp; Australia 555 ft 0.13 in pp)
Beam: 80-ft (24.4-m) design, but varied slightly with *Indefatigable* and *New Zealand* being 79 ft 10.2 in and Australia being 79 ft 11.75 in
Draught: normal 27-ft (8-m)
Displacement: 18,740 tons normal and 22,430 tons fully loaded
Speed: design speed of 25.5 knots at normal draught; 26.9 knots achieved at forced draught during trials
Armour Protection: armour belt 6-in thick amidships tapering to 4-in forward (the belt extended to 3 ft 6 in below and 7 ft 6 in above the low water line); barbets were 7 in , main armament turrets were 10-7-in, conning tower 6 in aft and 10-in fore, and communications tubes between 3 and 4 in. The main deck was 1-in forward with lower deck 1.5 in forward sloping to 2 in amidships and 2 in aft.
Armament: as built a main battery of eight 12-in/45 caliber Mk X guns in four turrets – one forward, one aft and one on each of the wings; 80 rounds per gun carried. Secondary armament of 16 x 4-in (102-mm)/45 Caliber QF (Quick Firing) guns in single mounts with 100 rounds per gun. The class was built with 2 x 18 in (457 mm) submerged torpedo tubes. Additional armament could include machine guns and a number of small arms. Other armament added included 4 x 3-pounder guns and an AA (Anti Aircraft) armament of 3 x 3 in AA guns was added in 1915, although ships of the class varied
Complement: as designed 737, but normal complement was around 820, with this increasing to over 1,200 during World War 1

Appendix III

Lion Class

Length: 700-ft overall; 660 ft 0.5 in pp (*Princess Royal* length as built was 700 ft overall and 66 ft 0.81 in pp)
Beam: 88 ft 6 in design and 88 ft 7.4 in as built (*Princess Royal* 88 ft 6.44 in)
Draught: 28-ft (8.4-m)
Displacement: 26,350 tons normal and 31,324 tons full load – *Queen Mary* was 27,000 tons normal and 31,884 tons full load
Fuel capacity: coal 1,000 tons at normal load draught and 3,800 tons maximum; oil 1,000 tons
Speed: design speed was 28 knots; exceeded during trials
Armour Protection: 9-in main belt; 6 in upper belt amidships tapering to 5-in forward and 5 in aft (the belt extended to 3 ft 6 in below and 16 ft 6 in above the low water line); barbets 8-9 in, main armament turrets 10-7 in, conning tower 10 in and communications tubes 4 in. The main deck was 1-in over the citadel; lower deck 2.5 in fore and aft and 1.25 in amidships, 1.5-1 in funnel uptakes and 1-2.5 anti-torpedo bulkhead abreast of the ships magazines
Armament: the new main battery guns were built by Vickers for the new Super Dreadnought battleships with a main battery of 8 x BL 13.5-in/45 (343-mm) guns housed in four twin turrets – two four and two aft, with 80 rounds per gun. Secondary armament consisted of 16 x 4-in (102 mm)/45 Caliber QF (Quick Firing) guns and 2 x 21 in submerged torpedo tubes. Other armament carried included 4 x 3 pdr guns.
Complement: design 920, but normal complement was generally higher than this, reaching some 1,267 during World War 1

Note: Queen Mary had some noticeable differences compared with the Lion and Princess Royal

Appendix IV

Tiger

Length: 704-ft (215-m) overall; 660-ft (200-m) pp
Beam: 90.6-ft (27.6-m)
Draught: 28.5-ft (8.7-m)
Displacement: 28,490 tons normal and 33,500+ tons full load. Some figures of up to 36,000 tons have been put forward although this would never have been reached during the 1914-1918 war if at all
Speed: design speed of 28 knots (35-mph/56 km/h)
Armour Protection: main armour belt ranging from 9-in (230-mm) thick lower amidships, tapering to 6-in (152-mm) upper amidships and 3-in (76-mm) under lower armour belt, 9-in maximum thickness main armament barbets down to 8-in thickness; 9-in main armament turret faces, 10-in (250-mm) conning tower at maximum thickness, 2-in (51-mm) base, 3-in to 6-in over the roof, 6-in for torpedo control tower, 1-1.5-in (25-38-mm) deck armour, 4-in (100-mm) bulkheads, 4-5-in (100-130-mm) main battery bulkheads, 1-2.5-in (25-63-mm) magazine screens, 6-in (152-mm) front secondary battery casemates with 2-in (51-mm) at rear of casemates, upper forecastle 1-1.5-in (25-38-mm), lower amidships 1-in (25-mm) and 3-in (76-mm) lower bow
Armament: main battery of 8 x BL 13.5-in (343-mm)/45 Caliber Mk V guns housed in four twin turrets – two four and two aft, with 80 rounds per gun. Secondary armament consisted of 12 x 6-in (150-mm) MK VII guns, 2 x 3-in 76-mm guns for anti-aircraft role, 4 x 3-pounder (47-mm) light guns, around five 0.303-in (7.7-mm) machine guns and 4 x submerged 21-in torpedo tubes.
Complement: 1,109, but this increased during World War 1

Appendix V

Ship	Builder	Laid Down	Launched	Commissioned
Invincible	Armstrong Whitworth	2 April 1906	13 April 1907	20 March 1909
Inflexible	John Brown	5 Feb 1906	26 June 1907	20 Oct 1908
Indomitable	Fairfield	1 Mar 1906	16 Mar 1907	20 June 1908
Indefatigable	Devonport Dockyard	23 Feb 1909	28 Oct 1909	4 Feb 1911
New Zealand	Fairfield	20 June 1910	1 July 1911	19 Nov 1912
Australia	John Brown	23 June 1910	25 Oct 1911	21 June 1913
Lion	Devonport Dockyard	29 Nov 1909	6 Aug 1910	4 June 1912
Princess Royal	Vickers	2 May 1910	29 April 1911	14 Nov 1912
Queen Mary	Palmers	6 Mar 1911	20 Mar 1912	4 Sept 1913
Tiger	John Brown	6 June 1912	15 Dec 1913	3 Oct 1914

GLOSSARY

AA	Anti Aircraft
AWM	Australian War Memorial
BCS	Battle Cruiser Squadron
BEF	British Expeditionary Force
CS	Cruiser Squadron
E	East
ft	Feet
GMT	Greenwich Mean Time
Hm	Hectometre
HMAS	His Majesty's Australian Ship
HMS	His Majesty's Ship
HRH	His Royal Highness
IJN	Imperial Japanese Navy
in	Inch
LCS	Light Cruiser Squadron
LOC	Library Of Congress
N	North
N.E.	North East
N.W.	North West
Pdr	Pounder
QF	Quick Firing
RAN	Royal Australian Navy
RN	Royal Navy
RNZN	Royal New Zealand Navy
S.E.	South East
UK	United Kingdom
USA	United States of America
W	West
W/T	Wireless/Transmitter

BIBLIOGRAPHY

Records by Admiral of the fleet, Lord Fisher
Admiral Sturdee's Falklands Dispatch
Battle of Heligoland Bight Dispatch's
Battle of the Falklands report, HMS Kent
Secret G-69: Growth of British Fleet in home waters 4 August 1914 - 31 March 1916
Jellicoe's Letter of October 1914
The action off Heligoland, August 1914
The Battle of the Falkland Islands before and after
The Flight of the 'Goeben' and the 'Breslau,' an episode in naval history
The grand fleet; 1914-1916; its creation, development and work
The Harwich naval forces
The Naval Position in the Mediterranean.

In addition thousands of miscellaneous pages of documents and records ranging from diary extracts to ships logs have been consulted.

ABOUT THE AUTHOR

Hugh is a Historian and author and has published in excess of thirty books; non-fiction and fiction, writing under his own name as well as utilising two different Pseudonyms. He has also written for several international magazines, while his work has been used as reference for many other projects ranging from the Aviation industry, international news corporations, film media to encyclopedias and the computer gaming industry. He currently resides in his native Scotland

www.ingramcontent.com/pod-product-compliance
Lightning Source LLC
Chambersburg PA
CBHW080225170426
43192CB00015B/2753